SEEING IN THE DARK

The pastoral needs of blind and partially-sighted children and their parents

CHURCH INFORMATION OFFICE
Church House, Dean's Yard, London SW1

SBN 7151 0026 2

This book has been published by the
Church Information Office for the
Children's Council—one of the Councils of the
Church of England Board of Education

© Central Board of Finance of the
Church of England, 1969

First published February, 1969

Printed by the Church Army Press
Cowley, Oxford, England

Set in 12 pt Bembo typeface

Editor's Note

This is the fourth publication in a series of books published by the Children's Council dealing with the religious education of handicapped children. A group of specialists discusses the problems faced by blind and partially-sighted children, their parents and teachers. It is not possible adequately to help children towards spiritual maturity unless the real nature of their handicap is understood. The group has, therefore, set out to present the child, the provisions made for him by statutory and voluntary organisations and the ways in which religious education may be approached.

The Editor would like to express his sincere thanks to the members of the group, whose names appear overleaf, and also to Mr M. S. Colborne-Brown of the Royal National Institute for the Blind, and Mr W. Cunliffe of the Hethersett Centre for Blind Adolescents and to the many other persons who have contributed to the group's work.

A. H. DENNEY

Members of the Children's Council Working Party on the Pastoral Care of Blind Children

D. W. F. Folley, Headmaster, Lickey Grange School, Bromsgrove, Worcs.

E. R. Tudor Davies, National Society for Mentally Handicapped Children

Miss I. Shorter, Adviser in Religious Education, Diocese of Norwich

Mrs M. Bolton, School Teacher, Dorton House School, Sevenoaks, Kent

M. Bolton, Headmaster, Dorton House School, Sevenoaks, Kent

Miss J. Garling, School Teacher, Linden Lodge School, London SW19

Miss E. Fletcher, Tutor, College of Special Education, 85 Newman Street, London W1

F. H. Tooze, Sheffield School for the Blind, Sheffield, 10

Chapter 2 has been contributed by Mr M. S. Colborne Brown of the Royal National Institute for the Blind, and Chapter 6 has been contributed by Mr W. Cunliffe of the Hethersett Centre for Blind Adolescents.

Preface

The following paragraph was written by one of the members of the working group responsible for this book. It first appeared as part of one of the papers submitted, but so clearly expresses the aim of all members of the group that it has been placed here as an indication of the aim of the publication, and the reason why it has been undertaken.

'This little book has been produced by a small group of Christian teachers and others, with the wide aim of helping parents, parochial clergy, teachers and all who may come up against the problems that blindness raises. We hope that what we have to say will be useful to all, whether or not they accept a Christian interpretation of life; but we feel strongly that the value and purpose of all life and the living of life fully and completely by all, can only be understood and carried through in the light of Christian faith and with the help of the community of caring Christians.'

Contents

Contents (contd)

CHAPTER 1

Facing the Fact

In all of us there is an innate fear of the dark. It is not surprising that hopelessness and despair are equated with blackness, and the forces of evil with darkness. ' Loss of sight has always been regarded as the greatest misfortune that can befall an individual, next to loss of life itself. This common conviction is based on the dominant role which sight plays in the activities of man. As a result of the emphasis on sight, the blind person is regarded as most seriously handicapped, disabled and almost helpless. This attitude is supported by a process of conditioning which proceeds from early childhood on. Children are told in fairy tales of the poor, helpless blind man, then of the blind beggar, and later on cannot help but associate ' blind ' with ' poor and helpless '. Such an appraisal of blindness also leads the public to believe that the blind must be profoundly unhappy and their lives filled with despair and tragedy.' (Lowenfeld.)

It is natural, therefore, that parents of a blind baby will not only suffer a severe sense of shock but will also feel a sense of guilt. Some religious influences and naive concepts of justice, as well as super-stition, explain blindness as retribution for sin committed by parents and ancestors. Many people thus regard blindness in a child as punishment imposed upon the parents and blame them for the child's handicap. This attitude, even if the parents only assume that it is present in others, causes them to be ashamed of their child and may drive them into feelings of remorse. Not only may a parent feel guilty, but he will also feel helpless; it is most important, therefore, that parents should seek and be given advice as soon as possible. All experienced teachers of the blind know that blindness is by no means such a severe handicap as is often supposed and that an educated blind child can take his rightful place in normal society. Parents must be helped quickly in what to look for and what to encourage. Blindness does not *make* a child abnormal. The mother needs to see that except in respect of its sight the child is like any other and that he requires not only love and security but also the chance to become self-confident and to make the fullest use possible of all his chances. He must not be smothered with over-protection and over-indulgence. He must be encouraged to adventure and explore. He must be fed with the experiences that a sighted child picks up by visual imitation. There are a number of pamphlets published by the Royal National Institute for the Blind which parents of blind children may find of great assistance.

It is important from the outset that the Local Authority be aware of the existence of a blind child. It is hoped that the ophthalmic surgeon will register the child as blind as early as possible and that the family doctor will advise the parents whom to approach. The local Health and Welfare authorities and—from the age of two—the Education Authority can offer help and guidance, and this can be backed by the assistance of the local voluntary Associations and Societies for the Blind. Homes which have a child registered as blind will receive regular visits from the Social Welfare Worker for the Blind (previously called a Home Teacher) employed by the Local Authority.

It cannot be overstressed how important are the pre-school formative years for the blind child. Although residential nursery schools (Sunshine Homes) still exist, they cater mainly for the additionally handicapped child, for it has been recognised in recent years that the best person to care for the child is the mother. The head teacher and staff of the school for blind children in the area of the home will always be ready to give assistance. No doubt the parents will wish to see the school before the child reaches the age of five, and this may easily be done, either by personal arrangement or through the Local Education Authority or visiting welfare worker.

The shock for parents of discovering that a baby is not ' normal ' is tremendous, whether it comes suddenly and certainly at the moment of birth or as the result of an accident, or builds up gradually over a period of weeks or months of dread and suspicion. However the disability occurs or is discovered, the parents of a handicapped child need help as well as sympathy to become adjusted to the situation. How sad, and not infrequent, are the cases when parents find such a child utterly repulsive and are not only unable to face the situation but cannot accept the child and have no wish to do anything for him. Others are so unhappy and wretched that their fretting and misery has a bad effect on themselves, on the child, and on other children in the family. Even those who can accept the fact as something which must be dealt with usually have no knowledge of the right way to begin to care for a blind baby so as to give him the very best opportunities of growing up to live a full and happy life. Often those who are most anxious to do everything possible to help the child, make the great mistake of being overprotective and do far too much for him. These parents, too, need help and guidance.

Who is to help? Those who teach blind children in school and the social workers who help blind adults in a great variety of ways are often very aware of the importance of early training and of the irreparable damage that is often done before the child comes to school; but few of these people have an early enough opportunity of meeting and helping parents, and if they do, they have not the time to do more than talk briefly to the parents and suggest the right lines to adopt.

Parents are only free to help the child properly when they have struggled through the agony of becoming adjusted themselves to the fact that he is blind, and this is a struggle and an agony to believing Christians as well as to others. It is in grappling with this kind of suffering that many Christians learn to know the meaning of sharing the cross of Christ, and after the darkness and doubt there may well be a strengthening and renewal of faith which will see them through.

If the struggle is bitter for those with faith, what must it be for those without? The bitterness and despair of such people is understandable. Often clergy feel so inadequate that they stay away, keep off the subject, or show sympathy in a vague, kindly, non-committal way. Often people are helped if Christians boldly, and without apologising for doing so, make them look at themselves and their trouble in the light of Christian teaching and of other people's experience, with and without God's help and strength. Life is not going to be easy for this handicapped child, and if his parents can help him to know and trust in a God whom they know and trust, they will have given him the very best foundation for coping with life.

The priest or minister who wishes to help such people must be prepared to meet bitterness, a sense of guilt at having produced a blind child, and sometimes the complete rejection of the child by one or both parents because of the feeling of repulsion his blindness gives them. Above all, he will find that he is dealing with very lonely people. It is unlikely that they know anyone else in a similar situation, and it is nearly always a great help if they can meet someone who has faced it.

It is very important that parents should begin as soon as possible to learn everything they can about blind people. This will help them to see their problem as a challenge and as an interesting job to be done.

In the pre-school years and when the child is home during school holidays the parent has a particularly important role to play. What he sees stimulates a baby or young child into activity and into creating experiences for himself. In the cot he will reach for a rattle; he will crawl towards an attractive object; he will respond to what he sees in his mother's eyes and to the expression on her face. The blind child obviously lacks this visual stimulation and so extra effort is needed from the parents to compensate for this.

Blind children are often reared in an atmosphere of high emotional tension. The handicap seems so terrible to the parents that they react by feeling the child has much to bear and must, therefore, be given no extra pain or annoyance by being made to conform over matters of daily routine, but must be kept happy all the time. The child is thus denied the framework of loving firmness which would help him over many of his difficulties, and give him the comfort of knowing that his parents are wise and strong, and that he can relax in their tender care. When he is being fed sweetened milk from a bottle he is caught up in a state of sensual delight in his mother's arms, with no distractions; all too often cup and spoon feeding are not introduced early enough, when he would accept them as part of the routine. When he gets to a year or more his mother feels he should really be weaned, but by now he is unwilling to give up his intense pleasure in the bottle, and will not accept the cup or spoon against his lips. Now he is strong and he fights for his rights. His mother soon gives up and says to herself, ' He will come to it in time '. Hand feeding, too, is often delayed. It is thought that he cannot find his way to his mouth, and once he drops the food offered it is not put into his hand again—yet he cannot find it for himself. There is no play around hand-feeding as there is with the sighted child—' give Daddy a bit '—and he does not see other people hand feeding, so cannot instigate it for himself by reaching out and doing it. All children learn by observation and imitation (about 90 per cent. of learning in the young child comes through these processes). Since the blind child can do neither, the fragments of knowledge he gets through his other senses cannot be properly understood. The objects he feels and the sounds he hears are meaningless to him unless he is helped to associate them with certain functions, movements, or pleasurable experiences. Purposeful speech can be encouraged if his early attempts at phonation are turned into useful words like 'bang' and 'dinner', and other words such as 'up' and 'down' are illustrated by the movements. He has to learn that everything has a name.

There is a temptation to keep the child secure from harm in cot or pram. Thus many blind babies never learn to crawl and lack, too, many of the experiences which would help them when they arrive at school. For all children, purposeful play is the key to learning with understanding. Blind children, lacking the visual stimulation of their environment, need more direction. Water, cooking utensils, stones, in fact most of the everyday things of life are of far more value to a blind child than expensive soft toys or unrealistic plastic ones, for he can spend profitable and enjoyable time exploring their possibilities. The parents need help to channel their concern into taxing their ingenuity to provide motivation for exploration and experiment on the child's part.

At school the blind child will be encouraged to learn to stand on his own feet. He will learn to use his mind and his hands and to find his way about. It is important, therefore, that the school child be encouraged and helped to continue in the same way during the holidays. Many children will have been doing domestic science and so can help with the cooking and housework. They may have been out shopping and can be encouraged to do the same for mother. The child needs to be allowed to contribute something to the household. It is important that he should not be allowed to sit in the house, but be encouraged to go out to play and to explore his environment as far as safety permits. Parents can help to widen the child's experience by making visits to the market, taking him on escalators and in lifts, to interesting places such as museums in the locality. To be a part of the life of the local community will be very beneficial to the visually handicapped child.

Parents can become quite fascinated and immensely cheered by finding out how blind people learn, work, play and enjoy themselves in such a variety of ways, and in getting to know about all the equipment available—books, gadgets and helps of all kinds. It is often a good thing for them to begin to learn Braille long before

13

the child needs it, so that it is already normal and acceptable to them as a means of reading and writing, and they are equipped to write to their child and to read his letters when he goes to school.

All this they can find out by contacting the head of the nearest school for the blind to arrange a visit. Heads of schools are keen to have the earliest possible opportunity of meeting such parents to give them advice and direction about the bringing up of their child, to discuss any particular problems, and to give all the information and help which it is vital for them to have. Seeing the normality of work and play in a school for the blind should give fresh heart to anxious parents and knowing that this is something to which they can look forward for their child should encourage them in the sometimes difficult days of early training.

Parents of schoolchildren gain much from visits to the school on the special occasions when they can meet and get to know and chat with other parents about difficulties, discoveries and successes. They can do much to encourage, cheer and instruct each other, and this is, of course, a great benefit to parents and children.

So far in this chapter we have considered the situation of parents facing the fact of blindness in children who will suffer this handicap all their lives. These children will have problems, worries and frustrations as they go through life, and those who work with them must always be ready to advise in a tactful and useful way. But amongst blind people, we are likely to find the greatest frustration, bitterness, fear and spiritual darkness amongst those who lose their sight after early childhood—those who have seen for long enough to remember seeing and who retain a visual memory. It is these people who need most help, understanding and constructive sympathy if they are to become happy, adjusted people who will again enjoy life to the full.

Those of us who work in schools for the blind are constantly facing the difficulties of children who have had full or partial sight and through illness, accident or deterioration have lost it during school days. It is remarkable how such children are nearly always helped by coming to a school for the blind: the children in the school are usually very friendly and welcoming, and being with other blind people of their own age does a great deal to help in the difficult days of adjusting to unaccustomed blindness.

It is important that these children make good friends amongst the adults who work with them, for however bravely and gaily and quickly they learn to cope with the new situation of living without sight, there will be times for nearly all of them when they need a sympathetic and wise adult friend to whom they can talk freely of their fears and worries and feeling of bitterness. It is so much better for people to talk of their unhappiness than to pretend it does not exist and to keep it bottled up inside themselves. Handicapped children do much to help each other in this matter, and although it is usual for them to want to get right away from blind people when they leave school, the majority are only too pleased to meet old blind friends again to exchange and discuss problems and funny stories which no seeing friend really understands or appreciates.

It is unwise to ' talk religion ' to an adolescent going through the difficult days of adjusting to blindness. Sometimes such children are noticeably rather quiet in discussions in Religious Knowledge lessons, or may have a rather bitter outlook on life generally. This is not always expressed in straightforward comment on their blindness, but may be seen in their difficult attitude to authority, sex, the Church, the school, or almost anything. Cases of extreme difficulty are rare, and have to be treated with great patience, kindness and good humour. Sometimes adjustment can be helped by finding one line of interest or ability which can be developed and which may be a means of helping everything else to fit into place. One girl who lost her sight in her early teens and had serious home problems, expressed bitterness and antagonism to religion for several years at school, but she showed outstanding ability in domestic science; probably because of her keen visual memory, she was quicker and more able than the rest of the class; much was made of this, and she reached a high standard of proficiency with a good examination pass in cookery: this did a great deal to help her general attitude and adjustment. Many similar examples could be given where some little thing has proved to be the anchor in the storm, and the means of coming to terms with blindness and being able to live a full, rich and happy life. Generally speaking, blind people are not unduly unhappy because of their handicap, and children in school are very amused when visitors remark with surprise at the atmosphere of gaiety and fun; the usual comment when these remarks are overheard is 'Why, what did they expect? Did they think we would be miserable? '

CHAPTER 2

The Pre-School Child

However much a family may ultimately accept (or seem to accept) their child's blindness, and welcome the services which we offer, we must always remember that no family wants a blind child in the first place. For most families it is, at the onset, a disaster: it isolates them, makes their child 'special', puts him into the world of hospitals and clinics, separates him from other children. It subjects them to conflicting advice and emotions: it arouses pity, guilt, overprotection. It imposes sudden, and considerable strains on the whole family relationship.

It is not surprising, therefore, that early help is needed—but it may not be welcomed unless we are able to understand something of the family's distress and confusion, to be tolerant of what may seem to be resentment and mismanagement, and to approach them with discretion and humility. We must not seek to impose our 'expert' knowledge, but must first win their confidence on a human and natural level, and see their problem. We must allow time—time for listening, as well as talking: we must realise that this is a totally new situation—they have probably never met a blind child before—and advice or information must be given slowly, in terms which they can comprehend, and which are meaningful to their own situation.

Ascertainment of the visual defect

Blindness, or severe visual defect, in a baby will probably have been first identified through a hospital. It is worth remembering that the very act of 'going to hospital' is, in itself, a bewildering and shattering performance for many people: this, coupled with the discovery of a serious affliction such as blindness, can be profoundly disturbing. It is important, therefore, that this first identification is not merely a measurement or diagnosis of the visual defect, important though this obviously is. It should be regarded as the starting point for the family, from which a positive programme of help and action can be developed. The parents should be given information as to the nature of the visual defect, its extent, and the prognosis. If the blindness is not total, they should be helped to understand what sort of use the baby may now, and later, be reasonably expected to make of what sight he has.

In my experience it does not help to conceal or postpone the facts of a baby's severe visual handicap, as it is particularly in these early years that help is most urgently needed. Observation of the normal baby shows the extent to which sight, above all other senses, organises the fragmented experiences which crowd in upon him; if deprived of this sense, a fundamentally different régime is called for if the parents are to give the child every chance of full development within his limitations.

Registration with the Local Authority

In order to take advantage of the services that are available, a formality known as Registration has to be completed. Sooner or later all blind people wishing to have access to the services for the blind are examined by a consultant ophthalmologist, and a form B.D.8 is completed. This is the means by which the appropriate Welfare Authorities and, through them, the RNIB, come to know of the case: it also provides a valuable basis for research. It is sometimes felt, particularly with a young child, or if the visual defect is one likely to improve (e.g. cataracts) that there is a finality about this formal procedure which will be upsetting to parents. I can only repeat that, in our experience, it is more upsetting for parents not to know where they stand, and to be denied the help and services that could be available. In any case, there need be nothing permanent about Registration: it is simply a record of the visual defect at that date. It is a frequent occurrence to find the B.D.8 altered later, or the child removed from the register altogether. In any case of doubt, it is always possible to consult the RNIB and this is not infrequently done by medical social workers, or parents. Registration is not a necessary prerequisite for consultation with the RNIB, but it is necessary if services are to be used.

Services available

(a) The Welfare Department. What are these services, and what is the advantage of them? Every registered blind person, of any age, is the responsibility of the Blind Welfare Department of his Local Authority; and a trained social worker is the personal link between the Authority and the individual. After the age of five the Local Education Authority is responsible for the education, and possibly the subsequent training, of any child who can benefit from education, but the Welfare Department has an overall responsibility, right into old age, for the well-being of each blind person. For the baby and his family, more specialised services are available through the RNIB, which works closely with the Welfare Department, and the Health Visitor.

(b) The RNIB Parent Counselling Service. From many years of experience with blind children the RNIB has evolved a service of parent counselling which centres round the Parents' Unit at Northwood, Middlesex. This rather formal name is nothing more than a largish semi-detached suburban house, staffed by a former Sunshine Home Head and her assistant; it contains no special 'apparatus', nor anything that is outside the ability of a perceptive mother or handyman father. To the Unit can come the family with their blind baby: more often it is just the mother who stays, with father bringing and collecting her. The arrangements for the visit are made with the minimum of official fuss, but wherever possible the Welfare Department is kept fully informed so that everyone can work together.

Not infrequently it is the first real break that the mother has had since the birth of her blind child: if the child has handicaps additional to blindness (which today is increasingly common) this means that it is a wonderful relief for her. There is time to talk, and someone who will listen: someone, what's more, who has had experience of blind children. Perhaps it is the first time that the child has had the chance, in a stress-free environment, to explore, to discover stairs, to feed without pressures and anxieties about 'making a mess'. In the space of a few days the mother can learn the beginnings of how to teach her child the independence she will want him to achieve: or she may have learnt to realise the severity of his handicaps, and ways in which she can best cope with them. This is human, family

18

living—with some expert skills tactfully inserted: the result is invariably increased confidence and understanding.

In some cases it is more useful for the Head of the Unit to visit the family in their own home instead, form an assessment of the situation as it is, and give the best possible advice and practical help in the circumstances. Sometimes a visit to the Unit may subsequently follow. In either case the family will be given a number of simple pamphlets (if they have not already received these through the RNIB) which will help them to follow up what has already been said: and these may be supplemented by feeding charts, simple hints on toilet training or child care which are particularly relevant. In all of this, they are beginning to feel less isolated: they are hearing of other children, other families, with the same problems: they are beginning to see a positive way of dealing with the situation, instead of a passive one.

While the family is at the Unit, they will have a chance to visit the Sunshine Home Nursery at Northwood: other families, who may live too far from London to feel they can make this journey, may have had their first contact with ' the blind ' as a result of a visit from the Head of one of the five other Sunshine Homes, all of which are maintained by the RNIB.

(c) The Sunshine Homes. These Homes have moved far from their original purpose of forty years ago, which was not then out of place in the context of the social thought of the time, as a loving refuge for blind babies. Quiet meal times, linked hands to prevent little ones getting lost, floppy sun hats to protect the delicate faces— gradually the fresh air of the new ideas in nursery school education cleared away these protective (though well-intentioned) cobwebs. Play with natural materials, and learning at first hand through their use and contact: free exploration and experiment; living as a small active community; going home for weekends and holidays; the recognition that such schools can only be fully effective in partnership with the family: these were some of the features of the Sunshine Homes in the last two decades. There have been further changes since, not in their essence or philosophy but in the services they seek to offer. This has come about through three main factors—the growing recognition that, given good supportive help, the child's own home is first and foremost the best place in the early years; the development in primary schools for the blind of their

19

own kindergarten departments, which are geared to the needs of five-year olds; and, above all, the increase in the number of blind children with additional handicaps, often severe. Today, of the ninety children in the Sunshine Homes, two-thirds have additional handicaps, physical, mental, or both: their care and training calls for skilful and specialist attention, while their demands are often more than the average family, with the best will in the world, can satisfy without endangering the whole balance of the family.

In seeking to meet the problems of these additionally handicapped blind children, every effort is also made to maintain (in some cases, to create for the first time) a loving and accepting relationship with the family. As far as possible (and, distance apart, not all children can easily adjust to a double régime) the children go home for weekends, half terms, and school holidays: there is frequent contact with the family, and if the Head ever feels that the child (or family) is fretting as a result of separation, this is quickly put right.

Not many people can naturally accept a blind child *as a child*: it is even more difficult if the child is mentally retarded, physically deformed, unattractive. It requires a conscious effort from most of us, who can often find excuses for evading the personal challenge, or salve our consciences by putting money in a collecting box. Because of blindness, early development is slow: everything takes such a long time if it is to be done effectively, and within the child's terms of comprehension and capacity. To discover the way a handle opens the door; the connection between the slice of bread, the loaf and the baker's shop; to explore the legs of all the furniture; what is in a drawer or on a shelf: all this is a slow process at first, and demands great patience and forbearing of the adults. But it is the only way the blind child will learn. It is so much quicker for the parent to tie his laces or button his coat for him; but he will not learn that way.

One of the most important functions of the Sunshine Homes today is the assessment of additionally handicapped blind children. If there are additional handicaps, not only is this whole process of development further retarded but the handicaps may actively prevent certain of its stages. These handicaps may also be obscured by the more obvious handicap of the blindness: and their multiplicity may present a challenge which is more than parents can accept without skilful guidance. The Consultants who visit the Sunshine Homes each term have long experience of such children: the Head of the

Sunshine Home will already have visited the child and his family in their own home: medical records will have been followed up and investigated. The child will come into a Sunshine Home for anything from a week to a term, during which the staff will watch him—how he reacts to other children, to adults; what he can, and cannot, achieve; what are the effects of the other handicaps. Much else (often unsuspected) may emerge during this period of assessment.

When the consultant paediatrician visits, it is possible to give the parents some reasonably clear picture of the extent of the child's handicaps, what may be expected of him, and how best to manage his development. And the earlier in the child's life this can be done the better, because all involved then know what they are working towards and the material with which they are working. These assessments are arranged with the full knowledge and support (including financial) of the Local Authority, so that already there can be the closest association between all the statutory agencies—health, welfare, social, educational—which may be concerned with the future of the blind child.

It may be suggested, after the initial assessment, that the child will benefit immediately from a longer period in a Sunshine Home to establish basic milestones of development; or to overcome certain (maybe temporary) problems, e.g. feeding, sleeping; or because the severity of the handicaps call for special care; or to give the family badly needed relief. Some children need the nursery environment of the Sunshine Home later on, when they have begun to outgrow the opportunities which the family can provide but are not quite ready for the environment of their 'big school'. In any event, during this time, whether it be a matter of months or years, contact will be maintained with the family, through the Sunshine Homes or the Parents' Unit, and also through the RNIB. In this way the progress of the child can be watched and the programme of education or care which he needs can be forecast. At the same time the parents will have the opportunity of learning about the services available, meeting some of the people who will be concerned with their child's education or care, understanding more clearly what are his special needs. Besides the parents, there are relations and friends: it is important that they, too, should know and understand the needs and problems of the blind child and his family. The blind child grows up, and will eventually be absorbed into the sighted com-

21

munity at some level, so it is obviously desirable that the sighted community should know how to deal with this particular member—with informed sympathy.

There are some blind children so handicapped by cerebral damage that the blindness is almost incidental; it is certainly not the dominant handicap. The degree of their handicap will obviously present grave problems of management even in childhood: and thereafter they will probably need institutional care. Not only is this much more difficult for any family to accept, but the placement of the child is difficult because of the present inadequate provision (day or residential) for the severely handicapped. Even if the services available to any blind pre-school child are of little use educationally to such children, the parents can at least have the assurance that through consultation and assessment their child has had every opportunity to show any potential: they have had the chance to talk over their problems with workers of wide experience and have probably been helped towards an objective acceptance of the position.

Some families are able to provide for their blind child an environment which is entirely satisfying for him (and not over-demanding of the family) right up till the time when he goes to school. These will probably make only minimal use of the services outlined above, but it is as well that they should know they are there, if wanted. They should also be encouraged to find out as much as possible about their child's future education—to visit the school he is going to, to make contact with the officer in the Education Department of their Local Education Authority who will have the administrative responsibility for their child. Because the LA, in its several aspects, may seem to be more extensively involved in the care of a handicapped child than it would be for his normal sibling (and this area of education is, after all, defined as ' special education ') this does not mean that the family, or the neighbours, can lessen their involvement. If anything, the reverse is the case.

It is sometimes possible for a young blind child to go to a sighted nursery or infant school within daily reach of his home. Most blind children go to schools for the blind, but this is not obligatory: and a few are educated side by side with sighted children. This is not the place to go into the pros and cons of what is known as ' open ' or ' integrated ' education: but a blind child of at least average ability, with no additional handicaps and a secure background, will gain much from mixing fully with his sighted contemporaries in

22

his early years.   But it must at the same time always be remembered that whereas the sighted child will, inevitably, always be learning through the sense of his sight, the blind child must be deliberately helped to absorb through his other senses: he will not do this instinctively.   To say ' the blind child learns by touch ' is a half truth: he learns by touch only in relation to the experiences and environments which the skilful teacher or parent gives him so that he *can* learn by touch.

CHAPTER 3

Time for School

British Schools for the Blind have a long tradition and are very experienced in their specialist task. The first English school was opened in Liverpool in 1791 and in the next fifty years a number of schools were founded all over the country, at such places as Bristol, Liverpool, York and Birmingham. During this period there was no efficient system of reading and writing for the blind, and prospects of employment were slight. These establishments were therefore places of shelter rather than of education. They were founded by voluntary bodies from Christian or humanitarian motives and religious teaching played a prominent role. About the year 1830 Louis Braille published in France his alphabet to be read by touch; when its value was finally recognised in England, about the year 1870, this gave great impetus to the education of blind children in this country. When in 1893 the Elementary Education (Blind and Deaf Children) Act was passed, making education for blind children compulsory between the ages of five and sixteen, a pattern of efficient education already existed.

Since the 1944 Education Act, Schools for the Blind have followed the national pattern. There are primary schools at Liverpool, Newcastle and Sheffield, a secondary school in Manchester and schools with primary and secondary departments at Bridgend, Bristol, Sevenoaks, Liverpool, London and Birmingham. There is a comprehensive school for Scottish children in Edinburgh and three selective secondary schools in England: Worcester College for Boys, Chorleywood College for Girls and the Royal Normal College at Shrewsbury. The majority of schools are still controlled by the voluntary organisations which founded them. They are directly responsible to, and inspected by, the Department of Education and Science and the pupils' fees are paid by the Local Education Authority where the child resides.

It is not compulsory for a blind child to attend a Special school but under present conditions it is obviously beneficial for him to do so. With the exception of Worcester and Chorleywood, all the schools are mixed and have small numbers of pupils compared with

24

schools for the seeing. The number of educable blind children of school age is about 950. Of necessity, therefore, all schools are boarding schools. They were founded near the large centres of population and it would be difficult to provide efficient small units scattered all over the country for one or two children each. It would be costly to provide specialist teachers in day schools to back up the work done in the classroom and to teach braille, mobility and physical education, and the blind child in such schools might well feel isolated. In any case, there are positive benefits to be obtained from boarding education for blind children, provided that they are able to maintain regular contact with their homes. The Special boarding school is able to provide teachers expert in braille and methods applicable to the blind. Where all the children are visually handicapped, they can take part in games and activities which would be very difficult for them in the setting of the ordinary day school. The children can be kept occupied and introduced to varying activities in a way that a busy mother at home would find it difficult to do. The blind child will not be the centre of attention, receiving but perhaps not giving, when he is one of a resident community of similarly handicapped children.

The curriculum in the schools is identical with that in schools for seeing children. In the primary departments children are encouraged to discover and explore for themselves; they gradually learn to gain confidence in their own abilities and to find their way about. The process is continued in the secondary department, where school subjects are taught in a more formal manner. This may be backed up by visits to many places in the local community to see factories, law courts, fire stations, etc. All schools have gymnasiums, most have swimming pools, domestic science and craft rooms, and some science and language laboratories. The staff are all trained teachers who hold an additional qualification in teaching blind children. Many teachers are resident and give freely of their time to help organisations, clubs, and societies such as literary and debating societies or meccano, wireless or dancing clubs; most schools have their own games and uniformed organisations. The children are treated as individuals and their day to day needs, so far as clothing, food and someone to turn to are concerned, are met by house-mothers and domestic staff as well as by the teachers.

Apart from grasping a few concepts which are essentially visual, such as colour or perspective, the average blind child can keep up with or indeed excel his sighted contemporary in all spheres. Learning to read and write through the medium of braille takes rather longer than by sight, but once proficiency is attained the child quickly catches up. The intelligent blind child can take CSE, ' O ' Levels and 'A' Levels, and gain entrance to universities and colleges.

Many of the pupils in the grammar schools who go on to the universities then find their place in the professions. Many other children receive training before finding employment, for instance, in piano tuning or typewriting and shorthand at the Royal Normal College, or light engineering at the Queen Alexandra College at Harborne. There are two Assessment Centres for training and placing blind adolescents, at Hethersett and Harborne.

So far we have been talking about blind children without defining in any way the term ' blindness '. For educational purposes, blindness means that a child's sight is not good enough for him to benefit from education in a normal school. The amount and type of sight varies enormously, but the vast majority will need to learn through the medium of braille. There are also children who are visually handicapped but have enough vision to learn by special methods, using their sight. These children are termed *partially sighted* and attend Special schools or classes for partially-sighted children. Most of these are day schools maintained by Local Authorities and there is a partially-sighted school in most large centres of population. However, some children in rural districts and smaller towns have to attend boarding schools for partially-sighted children. The difficulties for the partially-sighted child may be greater than for the totally blind. His sight allows him to play and run about like other children and other people may not recognise that he is visually handicapped. The amount of sight may vary from bordering on blindness to practically full vision except for reading. If partially-sighted children can go to an ordinary infant school it will be to their benefit, even if they transfer to a school for the partially sighted at a later stage. The near blind child is in a more awkward situation, since no clear border-line can be drawn. The first recommendation for a school will come from the ophthalmic surgeon and the final decision will be made by the school concerned. But if there is any doubt, the head teacher of a school for the blind will usually admit such children, transferring them later to a school for the partially sighted if it is to their advantage.

CHAPTER 4

The New Environment

It is important that a child should be prepared for the change to the new environment of school, and that parents and teachers should have the opportunity of meeting before the actual admission date. The teacher will want to learn about the child from the parents, just as much as the parents will wish to be given information about the school. It is essential for the well-being of the child that home and school should work together, and each must respect the part played by the other. The boarding school is a home supplement, not a home substitute. A child's first loyalty will always be to his parents, but as he finds happiness in the school activities, and as he learns to trust the new people who are caring for him—his teacher and his housemother—he will become a more confident child, secure in his new environment, while parents will accept that this period at school is part of the whole plan of the children's lives—a preparation for a full and useful adult life.

Upon admission to the school a child will feel more secure if he brings from home one or two favourite possessions which he can keep in his bedroom, or in a personal locker in the playroom. The closest possible link must be kept with his home. Pupils in most schools for the blind are able to go home at weekends, when this is a geographical possibility, and of course all go home for the usual school holidays.

A child likes routine and responds to the normal, ordered, harmonious atmosphere of the school. This can be helped by parents being regular in their contacts, so that the child knows exactly when he can expect a letter or telephone call from home.

Blindness is the one factor which brings the children into a special educational classification, but it does not make them into a homogeneous group. They come from varying home backgrounds and have differing abilities and qualities of character; some are totally blind, while some have restricted or variable vision; some have been blind from birth, while others have lost their sight at a much later age through illness or accident.

The education of a blind child, although along similar lines to that of a sighted child, must be adapted to meet these special circumstances, and be geared to meet the requirements of each individual. It is therefore necessary to have small numbers in the classes and to have a higher ratio of teachers to pupils, to ensure the necessary individual tuition.

A visually handicapped child is limited in the ordinary range of experience, simply because his lack of sight prevents him from having the usual visual incentive to reach out and explore the object lying some distance away from him, or even from just asking questions about what can be seen to be happening some distance away. Every child should have appropriate experiences at certain ages, and likewise the blind child should be encouraged to acquire the skills of all children of his own age. Careful watch should be kept for signs of readiness, and the experienced teacher and housemother will give the children opportunities for both mental and physical exploration, helping the child to develop at his own pace and level without the anxious stimulus or over-protection which is often very naturally present at home.

A blind child cannot gain his sensory experiences through sight, and therefore he has to depend upon the other senses, which have to be trained. He must use ' touch ' in order to ' look ' with his fingers; he must use his ears to locate his whereabouts, and learn through experience the connection between a sound and the object making it. Play experience is an essential part of development in the early years—yet some blind infants have never learned to play. Blind children delight in ' making pastry ', washing-up after a tea-party of sweets and orange squash, and washing clothes. The sorting of buttons or coins is another activity which can be enjoyed and at the same time gives opportunities for strengthening muscles of fingers and hands, and for developing discriminatory touch. By being given the opportunity to handle a wide variety of materials, by having a variety of play and story activities to develop the imagination, by being introduced to new experiences and by using specially adapted equipment, the blind child can be helped to overcome many of the difficulties of learning.

Braille is the medium used for reading and writing. This is a system of embossed dots read by the pads of the forefingers. By using all combinations out of six raised dots grouped thus ⠿ , not only are the twenty-six letters of the alphabet covered, but also punctuation marks and many contractions. Letters which come together frequently in words, like *ch, st, ou, ation,* have a special sign: single letters stand for complete words—*b* for but, *c* for can, *d* for do, etc: words like *and, for, of, the, with,* have their own signs. It is necessary to use contractions and accepted abbreviations of words to help the speed of reading and writing, and to reduce the bulk of braille books. Even so, braille is much more bulky than print: one copy of the Authorised Version of the Bible, for instance, is seventy-four large volumes in braille.

The Perkins Brailler is the machine usually used for writing braille in schools. This looks like a portable typewriter, but has only six keys. The appropriate keys pressed at the same time produce the corresponding embossed dots on the paper to form a letter or con-traction. Even though this is a portable machine, it is too heavy for much carrying about. It is therefore advisable for pupils to learn, at a later stage, how to write on a hand-frame, so that they can take notes quickly on any occasion. This involves using a style, which is pressed down into the paper in the frame to produce the raised dots on the other side of the paper. In order that these may be read from left to right, they have to be written the wrong way round from right to left, when using the hand-frame.

Although braille appears to the sighted person to be a strange and complex way of reading, it is much more effective than the earlier systems which made use of raised letters. Some blind children are unable to develop a good touch, or have other learning difficulties, but most are able to become efficient readers. There are not, of course, as many books available in braille as in print, but the Royal National Institute for the Blind, London, and the Scottish Braille Press, Edinburgh, produce a wide variety of books, including fiction for all ages and interests as well as educational books. There are also available a number of weekly and monthly magazines, e.g. *Braille Sporting Record, National Braille Mail, Home Help* and *School Magazine.* Any blind person may apply to have free weekly copies of the *Braille Radio Times* and *Braille News Summary.* Pupils are encouraged to become members of the National Library for the Blind, so that they can have reading material available at home during holidays as well as at school in term time. Many of these books are brailled by voluntary transcribers, who have learned braille specially to give this service to blind readers. Students can have books in specialist subjects transcribed for them by the Students' Library of the Royal National Institute for the Blind. The present-day development in the recording of books of all types on to tape is a great asset to the blind student, who can use a tape-recorder to augment his braille reading. It has also meant that the Talking Book Library, using tapes instead of records, has been able to increase its service to the blind. This is a service which is particularly appreciated by the older person who is losing his sight and who cannot read braille.

Older boys and girls are also taught to use an ordinary typewriter, and most become satisfactory touch typists, enabling them to correspond with family and friends who do not know braille. Ordinary handwriting is attempted, but this is difficult for those who have been blind from birth. Many, however, can learn to write their own signature, and a few can write short messages in ' square ' or other simplified form of handwriting.

Schools for the blind keep up to date with modern methods of teaching used in ordinary primary and secondary schools. New techniques and approaches are adapted, and whenever possible applied in teaching all subjects to blind children. Visual aids, of course, are not appropriate, but more use is made of the wireless and tape-recorder, and first-hand experience is given whenever possible. Visits to local places of interest like the fire station, farms, market gardens, the church and local schools, as well as trips farther afield to museums and historical houses must be included in the school's programme in order to give real meaning to whatever is being studied in the social studies curriculum. Special apparatus can be purchased for use in the teaching of mathematics, science and geography, but some of the equipment used is devised and made by the teaching staff themselves.

The Royal National Institute for the Blind also produces specially adapted games—braille playing cards, sets of dominoes, draughts and chess, and jig-saw puzzles. Wrist and pocket watches, alarm clocks, barometers and thermometers, as well as many gadgets to help the blind housewife, are also available. Because of the very special nature of many of these articles, their production costs are high, but special concession rates are allowed to blind customers in this country.

The children can learn a wide variety of craft work to acquire skill of hand, which is an invaluable possession for a blind child, and to provide for the development of initiative and self-expression. Clay modelling, pottery, weaving, leather work, knitting, rug-making, canework and woodwork are some of these activities. Both boys and girls are taught domestic science, in order to help them to become fully independent in their homes. There are few special gadgets used in the cookery lessons, but cookers are fitted with braille Regulo markings. (This is something which any blind housewife can have fitted on to her own cooker by the local gas or electricity boards.)

Whenever a pupil shows musical ability, every opportunity is taken to develop this gift. Many learn to play musical instruments and find enjoyment in music making as well as choral work. It is a common fallacy to suppose that all blind children are endowed from birth with special musical gifts. Some undoubtedly are so gifted, but not because they are blind. Unfortunately some blind children also have defects in hearing, but most are able to develop their sense of hearing to the full, and this enables even those with meagre talent to show surprising musical ability and appreciation.

One of the greatest difficulties for the blind is that of mobility. Blind people are not able to lead a full life unless they can move freely and independently. Mobility training, therefore, has an important place in the schools' curriculum. By having carefully planned schemes, schools hope to be able to train their pupils to move confidently not only in the known environment of home or school, but also to face all the difficulties and hazards of street travel. If a blind adolescent is to be able to move in a straight line mid-pavement, detect and anticipate kerbs, detect obstacles and move at speeds equal to his sighted friends, he must spend time and effort in training. He must learn to use his other senses for this purpose—to recognise different shops by their smells as he passes, to appreciate the differing texture of ground under his feet. He will be helped in the techniques of using a white stick, but this independence of movement can only be achieved after he has gained confidence and enjoyment in movement. It is not possible to predetermine any definite stage of mobility to be reached or to state the maximum of which every blind person is capable, for the result depends on the make-up of each individual and his opportunities of having move-ment experience in the early years.

Young children are encouraged to enjoy movement through music and singing games, and to use the climbing apparatus, swings, see-saws, wheelbarrows, tricycles and other outdoor toys. Gymnastics, dancing, games, swimming, roller-skating and athletics are all included in the physical education programme.

Of all these physical activities swimming is the ideal recreational activity for the blind. In the swimming baths, blind children experience an unhampered freedom which is not so easily achieved in other forms of physical education.

Dancing is another enjoyable activity which also prepares pupils for social contacts while at school and in later life. Blind children must cultivate pursuits which can be shared by those with and without sight, for it is through the common enjoyment of mutual interests that they will be able to share more widely in the activities of their home communities. In the boarding school situation there are opportunities for developing leisure time interests, and every school has a large number of clubs and societies, organised by the pupils themselves, by members of the staff, and by voluntary helpers. Through these out-of-school activities, contacts can be made beyond the school community. The Scouts, Guides, Cubs, Brownies and Red Cross cadets all join in local activities and enjoy interchange of visits and joint camps.

Every effort is made to help the pupils to take their places without embarrassment in a world of seeing people. Training is given in matters of hygiene and social conventions. The selection and care of clothing, hair-styling and make-up are all important topics to the teenager, and advice must be given at school. 'Design for Living' is the name given to one school club, which meets weekly to discuss ways and means of overcoming the ordinary day-to-day difficulties like care of nails and good grooming, or more involved matters like fashion trends and social etiquette.

These are some of the ways in which blind children enjoy their life at school, and at the same time are helped to develop a social poise which will enable them to feel at ease in the company of sighted folk. But their future depends on how far the local community will accept them and give them a chance of leading a full, useful and happy life.

CHAPTER 5

Communicating and Practising the Faith

Those who are responsible for communicating the Christian faith to blind children must be aware of their real needs and problems. Whether we be parents, teachers, clergy or other helpful friends, we must show a sympathy and understanding which is not sentimental, but useful, practical and helpful. In common with all who are trying to help others to know Christ, we must show, not only in our direct teaching, but by our attitudes and behaviour, that what we are offering is something worth having, and something which really works.

Some blind children have exceptionally good memories, and can often repeat years later something which they heard when quite young. It is therefore of vital importance that at no stage do we teach anything which will later have to be unlearnt. However simple our teaching may need to be, for young children it must always be true, and must still hold good when more profound teaching can be grasped.

Little blind children accept 'on faith' the early lessons about God who made everything, Jesus who came to show us what God is like, and the Spirit of God at work in the world today. They probably pray to an unseen God more easily than do seeing children, who can see everything except God. They may ask difficult questions, but what child does not? Perhaps for some, whose early faith has been simple and unquestioning, the result may be all the more shattering when later they come up against the ideas of their critical teenage contemporaries.

Family and friends
The young blind child who grows up in an atmosphere of love and security, and is able to trust implicitly the words and actions of those

with whom he comes into contact, knows that he ' belongs ' in his own family, and will find it easier to trust a loving, caring God and to want to become an active member of his family.

For many seeing people, an awareness of God as the Creator, a sense of what is ordered and beautiful in the natural world, will come through visual experience. Parents, friends and teachers of blind children must constantly help them to become aware of the innumerable sounds, scents and textures of their environment. We must widen their experiences in every sphere, in order that they may know something of the wonder and beauty of life. Moments of joy and discovery may become occasions for spontaneous thanksgiving, anywhere and at any time, for God is with us at all times and in all places.

As the blind child grows, he will meet more people and seeing children. Social experiences, personal relationships, learning to give and take, are of prime importance to the often very self-centred blind child. Time and frequent opportunities must be made for him, even before he reaches school age, to help others as well as himself. From an early age blind children must learn to give and to share. So often they are on the receiving end, and frequently unthinking people add to this difficulty by their very generosity. Blindness tends to make a person often quite unaware of the needs of others. If we really believe that it is more blessed to give than to receive, we should try to help these children to develop an unselfish interest in other people and a desire to do things for others. They very probably need many reminders and suggestions before this attitude of serving becomes natural to them, and those whom they seek to serve will need some teaching on the subject of handicapped people being able to serve as well as be served. It is important, too, for the child to use the gifts with which he has been endowed and to develop creative activity that will enrich both his own life and the lives of others.

Whose fault is it?

Sooner or later the children must face all the problems that blindness can bring. If they do not ask the questions themselves they must be asked to consider them and there must be complete honesty in answering them. The question asked by Jesus' disciples as they passed a blind beggar on the roadside, ' Lord, who did sin, this man or his parents, that he was born blind? ' is still a question burning in the hearts of many parents of blind children, and is constantly thrown at them by friends and relations in such remarks as ' I don't know what you've done to deserve it '. The blind children concerned are all too often treated by parents and friends as if they were not there, or had no hearing or feeling, and frequently they hear this question raised. They become uncomfortably aware of their parents' feelings of guilt and shame, and sense something of it too. We must face this question with the children and try to show them that neither blindness nor any other handicap or illness is a punishment from God. In many primitive religions, and indeed in the Old Testament, this is often thought to be so; and how glibly will people quote the Old Testament on the matter as if it were God's perfect revelation of himself to man! Jesus taught most clearly (and particularly on the occasion already mentioned in John, chapter 9), ' Neither hath this man sinned nor his parents, but that the works of God may be made manifest in him '. Blindness may result from such evil causes as disease, illness, carelessness (our own or someone else's), accidents, etc. God has given man freedom to act as he chooses, and all evil is ultimately the result of man's sin and is contrary to the will of God. We cannot blame God for our blindness; luckily very few people can blame anyone in particular, but we can accept the challenge that it is like any other difficulty in life, worth while overcoming; and it can become for us the very means by which we serve God the better through our successful overcoming. Without needing to receive physical sight, we can become like the man St John tells us of, someone through whom the works of God are shown to others.

Does God care?

The question 'Why, if God is wholly love, as Jesus taught, does he allow so much suffering? ' is one which puzzles us all, and of course, parents whose children are born blind and children who lose their sight gradually or suddenly after having seen, must ask this ' Why? ' Along with this question comes one about miracles. Why did Jesus heal so many people, being moved with pity wherever he went? Why does he apparently not care about us? What about faith-healing today? We must not avoid facing and discussing these difficult questions, but if we have no answer we must say so. If we understood everything we should be as God. St Paul's phrase in 1 Cor. 13 about now only ' seeing through a glass darkly ' is a comfort to some. St Paul himself is a great example of one who lived with ' a thorn in the flesh ' as he described it. This may have been poor sight. It was not miraculously taken away from him but he lived with it, and much other suffering too, and was happy to do so. Such was his devotion to Christ, that nothing could separate him from his Master or stand in the way of his serving him.

Can I be cured?

Much harm can be done to a blind child by ignorant adults who, whatever the evidence to the contrary, tell him that one day he will see. Sometimes they even state a particular age to the child. This can do nothing but harm. Nothing could be worse for destroying a man's faith in God, in people, in everything, than the disappointment when this hope is not realised. It is far better for a child to know he is blind and to expect always to be so, than to face this disappointment. When a child has to undergo an operation which may restore some sight, care should be taken to see that he is given no false hope. When an eye has to be removed, if the child is old enough to understand, he should be told that the eye is bad, and would be harmful to his general health if it remained; but a child without eyes should know that he will never see.

The question of faith-healing today is a difficult one, but one which blind children are usually eager to discuss. Here again great harm has sometimes been done to the faith of blind children who were given hope of sight and nothing happened. We must always make it clear when discussing any form of healing which is possible today, that for some reason which we do not understand it is always only a few who receive healing. It is far more helpful and constructive to teach about the help and strength which God gives us to face and overcome our difficulties, than to dwell too long on worrying about how to get rid of them. Our task is to confront children with Jesus and to help them to know him and to see him who is invisible to human eyes.

Learning and teaching

The methods we use in trying to bring the faith to blind children differ very little from those used in the teaching of seeing children. Our religious knowledge lessons, the special teaching and worship of particular Churches, school worship, intimate and informal discussion amongst children and with adults, must all be used together to bring a living experience of the Christian faith to our children.

Those particularly responsible for the teaching of religious knowledge in schools for the blind should, like the teachers of other subjects, be aware of the current trends in the education of sighted children and should try to work along similar lines. Our general educational principles are the same for all children, and the methods we use in schools for the blind must approximate as nearly as possible to those used in ordinary schools.

At the time of the writing of this book much fresh thinking is going on about the way religion should be presented to children. In the past, teachers thought they were giving religious instruction if they simply told and retold certain Bible stories which were good stories and appealed to young children. Not enough thought was given as to their value in conveying to the children any knowledge or understanding of God. Before the child reached the senior school he had dismissed Baby Moses, Joseph's coat of many colours, Baby Jesus, David and Goliath and so on, as fairy tales which he had now grown beyond.

Pioneered by Dr Ronald Goldman, the new approach sets out to help the child to find out about God: his dependence upon God and his responsibility to God, and the interdependence and mutual responsibility of all God's children to each other. It is now realised that the best way for a child to begin to discover God is not in stories of ancient Hebrews but by learning to see God at work in every-day life situations.

Religious education is inseparable from the whole learning process, and the child is constantly being given opportunities to find out about the world around him. Whether his discoveries be of a scientific, social or aesthetic nature, they are all part of the world which God created, in which his family lives, and each of us is a member of this family.

Life themes

In the thematic approach to religious studies which is being widely used today, themes springing from the child's own experience show God at work in our world. Thus the study of homes, family life, bread, water, spring-time and harvest, will help the child to understand our dependence upon each other and on God's laws of nature. A blind child who has already had the experience of helping his mother with cooking, cleaning and shopping, and has assisted his father in practical jobs of mending and making about the house, will be well prepared for this kind of teaching. If he has grown seeds in his own garden, visited a farm and been allowed to handle the animals and ride a donkey, and has kept his own pets or helped to look after a baby sister or brother, he has experienced something of loving and caring for others with its responsibilities and rewards. Suitable Bible stories may be introduced where relevant; these should not be read from the Bible, but should be carefully told, with background information, chosen according to the age and previous knowledge of the children, added to give meaning to the story.

The human Jesus
At the same time a simple life of Jesus may be introduced to quite young children, with interesting detail about the country and the way people lived and worked then. This could be introduced by means of comparison between the child's own life and that of the boy Jesus.

The life of Jesus can be brought closer to our life today by relating it to our observance of the Christian festivals, especially Christmas and Easter, and these can be made more meaningful to a child when they are related to the birth of a baby to someone he knows or to the yearly miracle of spring.

Bible themes may be introduced to older Juniors, such as ' How the Hebrew people learned about God ', or ' How they worshipped God '. More can be learnt about Jesus and his friends, but as junior children are not able to think in abstract terms, much of the ethical teaching of Jesus must be left until a later stage. They can learn something of Jesus' method of teaching by telling stories, through such parables as the lost sheep, the prodigal son and the good Samaritan, as the lesson and application of these is fairly easy to see. Junior children are inspired by stories of Christian heroes throughout the ages—of Jesus' friend Peter, of St Paul and others, including those of our own day who travel to remote and dangerous places to take the good news of Jesus to others. Stories of those who have worked for the needy in difficult and unpleasant conditions will also confront children with Christian qualities, and help to show them that Christianity is a way of life.

This method of religious education is made interesting to sighted children by visual aids of all kinds and many things for the children to do. It is often difficult to find useful and meaningful activity for blind children, but teachers are always on the look-out for opportunities for the active participation of the children. Throughout much of their learning they can make models, using a variety of materials; they can write prayers and praises, and act stories, preferably dressing up in costumes as nearly as possible like those worn by the original characters.

Because classes are small and teachers and children are usually resident in schools for the blind, and know each other well, discussion plays a large part in every subject. By the time the children reach the senior department of the school, their religious studies should be as wide and all-embracing as possible. Religion should be seen as part of everyday life, and as having an important part in aesthetic and social studies. To take one example, it is good to discuss the problems of other handicapped people and to consider the mutual responsibility and interdependence of all people. In all schools for the blind the children are encouraged to help the underprivileged. Annual harvest festival services are held and the produce distributed locally to those in need, sales of work and concerts are given to raise funds for natural disasters and good causes. The juniors in one school make a habit of getting up little plays, concerts and 'fashion parades' in the dormitories and performing them to duty staff—any money put in the hat is then sent to a cause of the children's own choice with an accompanying braille letter. Sometimes school choirs or groups give concerts in local churches, old people's homes, or mental hospitals, thus learning to give their own time and talents. Many blind pupils contribute money regularly to such organisations as War on Want, Oxfam, or the Save the Children Fund. This is made more interesting and meaningful to the children when support is given to some particular school or person. In some cases a link has been formed with a needy school for the blind in another country: parcels of suitable materials and braille books are sent out from time to time and some correspondence is maintained.

The Bible and Life
Adolescents have a need for security and what they learn must have some significance for them. They are beginning to form their own

very definite standards by which they measure other people and their ideas. Bible themes following on from those already studied may include such topics as:

Old Testament:
What is the Bible?
How was it written and put together?
The attitude of the Jewish people to race relations
The way God prepared his people for the coming of the Messiah
New Testament:
Jesus' relationships with people—with individuals and groups
The disciples learning about God from Jesus
The growth of criticism from those who opposed Jesus
Peter's story about Jesus (St Mark's Gospel)
Christian Living as Freedom and Fellowship (using Acts and Epistles)

In the last years at school studies might be made of such questions as:
The Church—its worship and fellowship
What it means to be a Christian
Prayer, Standards, Service, Responsibility for mission
The problems of living a Christian life

Thinking things through
Our children must, like all young people today, face, discuss and make decisions about moral issues. There is much good material in print to guide teachers, such as the SCM pamphlet *Thinking Things Through*. Questions such as attitude to work, the right use of time and money, fair play and honesty, the colour question, sex and marriage, etc., should be freely and frankly discussed. Often blind adolescents have not a very realistic understanding of what life is really like beyond their sheltered upbringing, and they should be made fully aware of the moral dangers they will have to face out in the world and be well prepared to meet them. It is a good thing for them to consider the difficulties which face blind people in marriage, especially when two blind people marry each other, and they should think out the problems of blind parents bringing up seeing children.

If a particular group of children are rather hostile to religious teaching and feel that people are 'getting at them', it may be wise for these moral questions to be studied under a different name, either in school time, or as an out-of-school activity. This might be called something like ' Social Studies ', and could perhaps include talks and discussions with such people as the school doctor, a child psychologist, a magistrate and many others.

Social themes which might be studied are: poverty and wealth, leisure, loneliness, responsibility for old people, mass media and communications.

The pupils might pursue particular interests and make particular investigations, perhaps working in pairs to gather material from books, radio, other people or from their own experience. They may run debates, write and produce scenes and sketches; they may meet people of other faiths and make a study of other contemporary religions. It may be possible for them sometimes to attend services at different Christian Churches. This could involve some preparation beforehand, and discussion afterwards.

Where it is desirable and suitable, this approach can lead naturally to the taking of CSE or GCE examinations for a few pupils. The facts learnt and the encouragement given to the children throughout the years to think for themselves will be a good preparation for the study of an examination syllabus and for answering the questions set on it.

School worship
Head teachers endeavour to make the daily school assembly a time of real devotion and worship, but much thought and imagination need to be given to keep it real and alive and meaningful. Hymns that make sense, with interesting music and keen choir work, can help. A theme running through hymn, reading and prayer helps to give purpose and meaning to the service. More participation by children is often a way of obtaining their interest. They may choose and read suitable portions of Scripture, choose and write or say the prayer, play the hymn, or perhaps—in groups—plan a whole service. There may be a committee of senior children who help to plan and arrange school worship; or classes may take it in turns to be responsible for a week, or for certain days. This can do much to help children to see the meaning and use of religion in daily life. It can be a way of teaching them to find their way about and use the Bible—no small task, with its many braille volumes! They can be encouraged to take an interest in music and can suggest suitable

music for quiet listening and thinking in worship, as well as music which they can perform.

Children and Church

As blind children are almost always resident at school for most of term time, provision should be made for them to receive instruction in the particular teaching of the Church to which they belong. The Roman Catholic Church usually makes adequate arrangements for its members, as regards both instruction and church attendance: other denominations are usually willing to help if approached and told what is required. Seldom do parents ask for a child to worship at a particular church, and even more rarely do they ask for him to be instructed in any particular faith. The ideal situation is for children to meet in groups with a member of the school staff who attends the same church. Teaching and discussion are easiest amongst people who already know each other well, and a teacher who is used to blind children will know the particular practical points over which to take special care. If it is necessary for this instruction to be given by strangers, it is helpful if they can find time to take some small part in other school activities, so that they and the children can get to know each other. Blind children should be given every possible help and encouragement to become adult members of their churches whilst still at school. Life is not going to be easy for any of them, and it will be of great benefit if they can develop spiritual resources. Belonging to a church can also be a means of making social contacts, which is often not easy for blind adults. The Christian faith must be seen as something which gives wholeness and meaning and gaiety to life, not as something dreary and forbidding. Blind children are as easily put off religion as any young people, and as hostile to anything which is advertised as good for them. Not only should they be given sound, clear teaching which makes sense to young people today, but they should also be allowed to discover all the detail which they might miss through not seeing. Clergy and ministers can help by letting children frequently visit and explore their churches. They should be allowed to handle everything and ask questions freely. This can be used by clergy as a means of getting to know individual children and the children can get to know them, too, as real people and not just as strange, often rather artificial voices. It is interesting for children not only to find out about the buildings, ornaments, furnishings, and clothes worn

42

by the clergy and choir, but also to be shown where people stand and what they do at various points in the service: how the collection is taken, what happens to it, and many other such practices of that particular church. We often forget how much of these little things blind people miss. Children should be helped to do as others do in church, and shown when to kneel, stand or sit.

When children are preparing for confirmation and Communion, careful instruction and practice should be given in the manner of receiving Communion by someone who finds no embarrassment in doing this down to the most minute detail. First they should learn the practice of the particular church which they attend, and, if this is the Church of England where one meets so many customs, a broadminded teacher can do much to prevent future alarms and surprises by showing them other customs which they may meet. It is so easy for those who can see to pick up a custom which they have not come across before just by observing what others do; but a blind person can feel most foolish and bewildered in a situation for which he has had no preparation.

Sunday worship is often a very real problem in schools for the blind, for it depends so much on the aliveness of the services available at the local church. Sometimes children sit, stand and kneel through a meaningless service, enduring hymns which they do not know, or (even more irritating) hymns which they think they know but which turn out to be slightly different from the version used at school. The sermon is often long and boring and seems to say nothing to them. No wonder they stumble and shuffle away, thankful that it is over for another week. Head teachers, finding this situation, sometimes substitute a school service. This is often very much preferred by the children. But how are they to get any idea of belonging to a Christian community beyond the school? And what is to take its place when they leave school? Probably nothing! How lucky to find a live parish where members of the school for the blind are welcomed by individual members of the church as individuals, where they feel they are fellow-members with them of the Christian community of the place, and where trouble is taken by all concerned to see that they can take their full, active part in the service. Some children may like to make their own copies of hymns and have a loose-leaf folder so that they can just take the hymns for that particular service. These can be dictated quite quickly during the week. In this way children soon build up a

43

collection, and by the time a complete year has passed they will find many repeats. Small copies of unchanging parts of the service may be taken, so that all can join in, but these are very soon unnecessary as they are quickly memorised. Music teachers may help by teaching some of the frequently-used church music. If there is co-operation between clergy and teachers, help can be given by the putting into braille of carefully chosen material, especially at the time of confirmation. It is not wise for a crowd of blind children to take a great quantity of braille to church. This can be rather disturbing and distracting to people, and quite a nightmare to teachers responsible for getting children to and from church. Half an hour during the week to prepare for Sunday's service can do much to give it value and meaning.

It is not very easy for children to join very actively in the social life of the parish whilst still at school. Sometimes the experiment has been tried of senior blind children joining church youth clubs, but the relationship between the blind and seeing can be strained and unnatural. Greater success has been achieved when this has been done on an individual basis rather than with groups, but some probably do better to wait for this kind of activity until they have left school. Blind schoolchildren have sometimes joined local Sunday school classes, but inexperienced Sunday school teachers have often no idea how to treat them; it can become a rather amusing session for the blind, and something to be dreaded by the poor young teachers.

Good Bible teaching will prepare any who wish to do so to join study groups when they leave school and to be useful members of such groups. Some may join choirs and other church groups according to their interests; these can be valuable ways of having contact with people, and can give some variety and interest to life apart from daily work.

Growing in the Spirit

Little has been said so far about giving the child opportunity to develop his own spiritual life. Whether we are Christians or not, we must recognise that man has an aspect of his being which is beyond and superior to anything found in any other animal; and just as we feed and nurture the mind and body to get the best possible development and use of these, so should the spirit of man be given every opportunity, help and encouragement to grow.

So far in our dealing with the practice of religion we have been mainly concerned with the corporate worship of the school community and its integration into the wider Christian community.

Many young people today find the language and expression of the traditional worship of the Christian community dull and meaningless to them, and this often puts them off organised Christianity. When this is so it is all the more important that a personal spirituality should have the chance to develop, as this may lead later to an awareness of the need for corporate worship.

In any residential community there is little opportunity for quiet and solitude and time to think. The children in our residential schools work, play, eat, sleep, and often even bathe in the presence of other people, day after day, for between ten and fifteen years of term-time. This continual presence of others and the noise of record-players, radios and tape-recorders, make the likelihood of there being time to spend alone and quiet very remote.

The subject of prayer may be discussed at all levels, from infants to seniors, in classrooms and informally, but the opportunity to pray may be difficult to find, and the inclination may be even more elusive.

Little children may say prayers together in dormitories as some do with their mothers at home; they may have formal or informal prayers, perhaps some aloud together and some little moments for talking privately with God and thinking about things quietly. Whether this is done or not and how it is done, will depend, as it does at home, on the inclination and ability of the person in charge, for it can only be done by someone who can participate with sincerity and meaning.

If the habit of saying prayers together stops suddenly at a particular moment of growing up and changing dormitories, children are very likely to think they have reached the stage in growing up when they no longer need to say prayers. Just as at home, mother should gradually take less part in children's prayers, and should sometimes suggest that her child says his prayers without her, so children at school should be gradually weaned from the direction and assistance of an adult. Probably in the early junior years it could be suggested that children pray or think quietly to themselves after 'lights out'.

To continue to provide a set 'quiet time' in dormitories for adolescents is quite useless, and is in fact dangerous and harmful. It either results in the mockery it deserves, or in a sanctimonious performance abhorrent to God as is the practice of Pharisees of all ages. The naturally religious blind child often needs fairly severe treatment to help him not to develop into this type of sanctimonious Christian. In these days when most residential schools are set in beautiful spacious grounds, the best thing is to suggest that children do their thinking and praying in the woods or fields or in the branches of a tree. Sometimes a school chapel or local church may be available.

From an early age children can be helped to develop a wide and vital concept of prayer. Those who are put off by the language of Church are not likely to find much meaning in the reciting of prayers in a language which is not their own. But a study of various prayers that have been used through the ages and of some translated from other languages can encourage in children an interest in the whole concept of prayer, what it means, and how it is best practised by us today.

It is necessary to give children some help and guidance so that they can grow from the childish ' saying of prayers ' to an adult life of prayer. It is not uncommon to find grown-up people whose notion of prayer does not extend beyond the simple words learnt at their mother's knee. The recently published book of *Children's Letters to God,* most of which seem to begin ' Dear God, I wish . . .' is a pathetic example of the wrong kind of start.

In starting discussions on prayer recently with a group of sixteen-year-old blind people, many of fairly high intelligence, it was interesting that the first few thoughts that came from them got no further than to suggest that prayer is asking and thanking. It was exciting to see how the whole group became alive and interested when a boy who is very small for his age, and usually thought of as being very slow, said quietly, and almost to himself: ' Prayer is a relationship with God '. Suddenly everyone became aware that we were talking about something real and vital, and many helpful ideas were put forward. When a big tough lad suggested rather shyly that a kindly thought was something very near to prayer he was much nearer the deep truth of the matter than he realised. If people think that prayer is just kneeling down beside one's bed at certain regular times and reciting set pieces, no wonder they see little point in it. If children have been brought up to be aware of God in the world around them, and in every situation of life, as well as in the Bible and in church, it should not be too difficult for them to grow up with an idea of prayer as a relationship with God. If we learn to think of prayer in this way, we know God to be involved with us in every aspect of our lives—our joys and worries, our relationships with others, and in the world situations. Prayer ceases to be thought of as asking someone a long way off for something you never get. In this close relationship the individual is working with God and with the others who are united in this fellowship, and God's help and strength are experienced more and more, the more we strive to perfect this relationship. This surely is the daily increasing in God's Holy Spirit referred to at our confirmation.

This inner life with God does not need much in the way of words, but it needs some time of quiet and peace in order that it may be experienced and bear fruit in the times of strain and stress.

It is valuable, at some stage, to show the various aspects of prayer—adoration, confession, thanksgiving, petition, and intercession; not that these may be gone through as a formal list, but that the whole range and richness of prayer may be experienced.

Older children should know about the kind of prayer that we call meditation and contemplation and should be encouraged to seek help and advice from experienced priests and ministers at all stages in developing their relationship with God.

The use of music, poetry, art, and all forms of beauty should be discussed as aids to spiritual thinking. Many people who do not claim to be ' religious ' are helped to deep thinking in a great variety of ways and by many means. Many Christians today are rethinking about the kinds of words used in prayer and the use of down to earth everyday language is helping many to make their praying something real and living. It is always difficult to get really up to date publications in braille; teachers can help to acquaint children with modern ideas and experiments by reading extracts from such books as *Prayers of Life* by Michel Quoist, and many others which depart so completely from the formal, stilted language which has usually been associated with prayer.

Maybe the fact that there are not endless books of prayers, leaflets, pamphlets, etc. in braille is an advantage, for seeing people are provided with so much literature that there is a real danger of reading prayers rather than praying. Those who try to help in this field should choose wisely and widely what they read aloud and what they put into braille, so that blind people may be helped and not hindered by the experience and expression of those who have found the inner life with God.

If all the opportunities are used, schools for the blind are ideal places for children to be brought up to be thinking people. The community is fairly small, and all activities are carried on by small groups of people similarly-aged. Many of these children grow up from early childhood to almost adult life together, and they get to know each other very well, and also their teachers and other adults who work with them. They learn sympathy and understanding, and a way of helping by living constantly with each other's difficulties as well as their own; they usually grow up to be people who are quick to know and feel someone else's need. Blind people are often great talkers, and there is much discussion on many subjects in these small informal groups, in the garden, in bedrooms, bathrooms, dining rooms—in fact all day long, in school and out of school matters, of all kinds are discussed. What an opportunity for Christians who work with these children, and what a responsibility to show Christianity in action, to talk with children and to bring a Christian point of view to their problems! It is important that such people show something worth while and that they demonstrate the fullness of life available to those who know Jesus. The more gay, attractive and up to date these people are, the more likely are the children to catch something of their Christian faith. It is often said that faith is 'caught and not taught'. This may be so for some in their first discovering of faith, learned from someone else, but for all of us there is need for much teaching and training too, if this faith is to mature into the vital reality behind everything in our lives.

CHAPTER 6

The Blind School-Leaver

The handicapped school-leaver faces all those difficulties which have also to be overcome by his more fortunate, non-disabled competitor. He has, however, to cope with additional difficulties arising directly from his handicap and where blindness is concerned these are considerable. First there is the frustratingly small range of paid work which can be done without sight. Thus it is often not a matter of finding something that one would like to do, but rather becoming reconciled to what there is to do. Secondly there is the difficulty of overcoming the ignorance or prejudice of employers about the capabilities of blind people. Pity and patronising admiration for simple achievements are readily given, whereas real trust in the performance of worthwhile tasks is begrudged, if not refused entirely, where business is concerned. This leads to a third difficulty, involving the amount of time required by a blind person to attain the usual speeds of performance. His relative slowness when taking instruction in practical matters is often regarded as proof that he will not perform the work to the required standard. Personal relationships with fellow workers are a fourth great difficulty. It is not easy to strike a balance between accepting reasonable assistance and proving one's independence. People often insist on giving unnecessary help, and when the due amount of gratitude is not forthcoming, then relations can become very strained indeed. As it is impossible to educate the whole of society in these matters, it is necessary for blind people themselves to be alerted to these dangers.

An obvious technical difficulty arises when a bonus scheme which depends upon team effort is in operation. If other members of the team consider that the blind member cannot maintain the average speed, his presence may well be resented by them.

For many years these difficulties were avoided by employing blind people solely at a limited number of crafts in special workshops for the blind. These still exist, but only a minority of blind people are so employed and particularly among the young there is a decided antipathy towards this segregation. Also, many of the crafts practised, are too difficult for the less able. In any case, the minimum age for the start of training in these workshops is eighteen, whereas the school-leaving age for blind children is sixteen.

These added difficulties in finding and keeping employment on the part of blind people have led to the creation of special machinery to assist them. The country is divided into several large regions by the Ministry of Labour, and a special officer, known as the Blind Persons' Resettlement Officer, is responsible for placing in employment all suitable blind adults resident in that area. Where juveniles are concerned, the Employment Department of the Royal National Institute for the Blind has a special responsibility throughout the country, and works in close liaison with the local Youth Employment Officer, who also has a duty to all young people in his district who are handicapped in any way. There are also special arrangements with the RNIB Employment Department concerned with commercial placements, and help at the professional level.

Ministry of Labour training courses for registered blind people are available in machine operating, typing, telephony, crafts, piano-tuning and physiotherapy. The final settling into permanent employment is assisted by a Training Officer, who actually works with the blind beginner for several days.

In order to take advantage of special provisions for the blind, a person must be registered as blind. For this he need not be totally blind but must ' not have sufficient sight to do work for which eye-sight is essential '. If he has more sight than this but is still severely restricted by bad sight, then he may be registered as partially sighted. This obtains some extra assistance from the YEO as a handicapped person but not the special provision available to registered blind people. There is sometimes difficulty when a child who is educated in a school for the partially sighted reaches school-leaving age. It may well be that if his sight is very bad, although he could manage in a special school for the partially sighted, he cannot hold employment as a sighted person. He may therefore transfer from the partially-sighted register to the blind register and avail himself of all the special arrangements.

Over employment, there is a distinction made between children attending grammar schools and those attending other schools. The grammar schools are visited regularly in connection with careers guidance and each school-leaver is given individual attention, whether it be for further education or direct placement in vocational training or business.

Academic qualifications obviously widen the field of possible employment for grammar school-leavers. ' O ' Levels qualify them for a place at the RNIB Training College for shorthand typists, recorder typists and telephonists, without the need for further education; also (preferably with the addition of at least one 'A' Level subject) for the RNIB School of Physiotherapy. Many blind men and women find physiotherapy a satisfying and worthwhile career either in private practice or on the staff of a hospital. A university degree—and a high proportion of Worcester boys go to university—may lead to one of the professions. The usual subjects studied are law, English, modern languages, history, music, mathematics, psychology or sociology.

Teaching is a difficult profession for the blind person. Many modern techniques taught in Colleges of Education are essentially visual, especially for the intending teacher of young children, but there are a number of qualified blind teachers in secondary modern and Special schools, and a degree will enable some to teach in grammar schools. A number of blind men with first class honours degrees are lecturing in various universities. In the past the two professions most usually followed by the blind were the Church and law. The former of these demands, of course, a special sense of vocation and few blind boys enter the Church nowadays. But the law can still be an attractive prospect, and there are many blind solicitors either in practice or on the staffs of large companies. Some old pupils of Worcester have taken up farming; one at least is in the Executive Branch of the Civil Service. A recent development has been training in computer programming for those who have mathematical ability. It is also possible for blind people to be trained as social welfare workers. Nevertheless, there are still many posts available to sighted grammar school-leavers which are closed to the blind. Careers in, for instance, medicine, architecture, engineering, surveying, the police and the armed forces are obviously not feasible. It is essential, therefore, that blind children should consider their future employment in relation to their handicap and not be encouraged to decide on careers which are going to prove impossible.

Where blind children from other than grammar schools are concerned, an interim stage between school and employment is available in the shape of a residential Vocational Guidance Centre, of which there are two in the country: Hethersett in Reigate, Surrey, and Queen Alexandra Training College at Harborne, Birmingham.

The three main aims of these Centres are vocational guidance, social adjustment and continued general education. Vocational guidance is given by introducing each student to all the types of employment open to him, so that he will have some practical experience on which to base his choice. The subjects included are: machine operating, industrial assembly, packing, crafts, typing, telephony and piano-tuning. There are also repeated interviews with a visiting panel, which includes the Employment Officer who will eventually place the student in employment. He is in close touch with these students throughout their stay at the Centre, and after their placement in employment he still remains in touch, until the student is twenty-one years of age. This continuity is most desirable.

Social adjustment is a deliberate attempt to assist the student to become independent and successful in his social relationships. This may in some ways be rendered more necessary by the fact that all schools for the blind are boarding-schools and therefore, in their school life, blind children develop in an unusual society. All their colleagues suffer from the common handicap of blindness. When they leave school, however, they must get used to a very different role in which they are required to fit themselves into a society which caters primarily for sighted people. There is a considerable amount of know-how which, when passed on to young people, can prevent much unhappiness and uncertainty later.

When blind children leave school it is felt that many are somewhat retarded educationally and, therefore, that general education should be retained in any training establishment until the age of eighteen. At the Vocational Guidance Centres it is necessary to introduce braille to newly-registered blind people as part of the insistence upon their use of senses other than that of faulty sight. It is also often possible to provide opportunities for taking standard external examinations, as a realistic comparison with the leavers from normal schools. As the Centres are small, with about forty students of only one age range (from sixteen to eighteen), the atmosphere is different from previous school life and thus enables an indifferent scholar to make what is tantamount to a new beginning without losing face. It is also possible to stress the aspects of education particularly concerned with the type of employment the student desires.

A real advantage of the Vocational Guidance Centre which might not at first be apparent, is the possibility which it provides of systematically conditioning the rather sheltered school-leaver for the work situation. Many of the less able school-leavers are very complacent about their state of affairs as regards employment. They are not aware of the effort required to reach the standard necessary for industry and are, in fact, at first quite unemployable. It requires a considerable period of stress on speed and accuracy in simple repetitive activities before the student realises what is expected of him and what he may expect of himself. To have to go through this process in normal industry is not a good thing, so that this period of preparation is invaluable.

Practical experience of industrial circumstances is also provided. Students go for a number of short fortnightly or three-weekly periods of trial employment at a variety of firms. This does much to remove the anxiety which is associated with one's first job. It also widens the experience of the beginner, so that the place where permanent employment is eventually found is not the only one in which the student will have worked.

During these periods of trial employment the student must satisfactorily make realistic journeys to and from work. He is, of course, prepared for this by being given instruction in getting about the streets and making use of public transport. This helps considerably when he seeks permanent employment, as many employers are anxious about the blind person's ability to get in and out of and about the factory.

Application for entry into these Centres must be made by the Local Education Authority in whose area the candidate lives. The Authority must then be responsible for paying the necessary fees. Further information can be obtained by applying to the Director General of the Royal National Institute for the Blind, 224 Great Portland Street, London W1, or to the Secretary, Birmingham Royal Institute for the Blind, Harborne, Birmingham.

CHAPTER 7

The Blind in the Community

We have tried to give a comprehensive picture of the work done by the home, the school, the assessment centre, and by many others, to help a young blind person to go out into the world equipped as fully as possible—mentally, physically and spiritually—to face the fun and the heartbreak, the elation and the frustration that full, active participation in the life of the community brings for all of us. The more opportunities a blind child has had of doing ordinary things with seeing people throughout his childhood and adolescence, the easier will it be for him when the break with the 'blind world' comes and he has to live day after day, at work and in his leisure time, entirely with seeing people.

Strange notions
Because the blind have been specially educated to come to terms with life in the seeing community, they will sometimes forget that seeing people have not yet been taught to come to terms with them. Speaking of his adjustment to the seeing community, a young blind person had this to say: ' People find it hard to understand that there is nothing wrong with me—except that I cannot see! '

Those who have never come in contact with blind people often have very strange notions about them. They are quite convinced either that the blind—all of them alike—are endowed with gifts and abilities far beyond those of any seeing person, or that the opposite is true and they are quite helpless imbeciles. It is difficult, in either case, to drive home the fact that the truth almost always lies somewhere between the two extremes. Many blind people have no other peculiarity except their blindness, but they differ from each other in their likes and dislikes, temperament and ability. It is quite usual for uninformed people to be certain that the blind are musical, have other senses augmented to make up for their blindness, and have phenomenal memories. In fact, some blind people are quite unmusical, some slightly or even severely deaf, and some are unfortunate enough to be absent-minded. But of course if a blind person is musical, it is good that he should make the most of it; if he has normal hearing, he uses it to the full and listens and interprets sounds in a way that is not necessary for seeing people; and it is wise for him to train his memory to full capacity, so that he need not always be burdened with the bulky equipment for reading and writing braille.

Those who are quite convinced that all blind people are without any normal ability to communicate will enquire after their health, or ask if they take sugar in their tea, through a seeing companion or parent. A little thought here would save many blind people much annoyance, and would make it less necessary to draw attention to their disability—something that the majority of handicapped people hate more than anything else. Stories of the thoughtless, foolish remarks of seeing people do, of course, provide food for much merriment when blind friends get together and exchange experiences. It is at these times that the story of the stupid woman can be laughed about—the woman who, instead of asking her blind guest the question, turned to her companion and asked 'Do the blind like pineapple?' Situations such as this led a distinguished blind woman to exclaim: 'Oh, how I wish that sighted people could put themselves—just for a moment—in our place!'

They never joke with a blind person

A blind housewife, with two small boys, said: 'People seem afraid to start a conversation with me, they never joke with a blind person!'

It is not always possible to relieve the tension between the blind and the seeing with a joke. A boy of sixteen, blind since childhood, said: 'If you try to take sugar from the ash tray, instead of the sugar basin in the café, people think it's sad, not funny....'

As with other kinds of handicap, it is often easier to joke with children than with adults; a blind girl who had worked in Thailand told a charming story about a group of seeing children she had met there. The subject was burglars; she had told them she was not afraid of thieves, because no one would wish to steal braille books. Back came the reply: 'Oh, but he might if he was a blind burglar!'—only to be followed by the further thought that even this might not be wise, because he would not be able to see the policeman coming.

Talking of a party she had been to, the housewife quoted above said, ' My host and hostess did not make an issue of my blindness. We talked on equal terms. There was no nonsense about anyone being marvellous.' It is very gratifying for the blind to find themselves taken for granted by the seeing community, but blind people can be tactless too, and it is sometimes their off-hand manner or downright rudeness which causes offence and embarrassment. They will see the natural ignorance and diffidence of the seeing as a stick to beat themselves with. A teacher, speaking of a man with whom she had once worked, said: ' He was so hostile to the seeing community that many who knew him would run a mile rather than have anything to do with a blind person.'

There are difficult people in all walks of life, in both the sighted and the unsighted world. Yet the blind person will, in general, naturally wish to seek and to keep social acceptance, and will only become reclusive and aggressive should he consistently fail to achieve this acceptance. To be socially acceptable is very important; it is often more difficult, and needs more hard work and thought, than does merely working at the job for which he has been trained. A young blind woman said, ' Our blindness makes us queer enough; we should make every effort not to have any other peculiarities.' This is a matter to which every blind person should give much thought. They should ever be watchful to guard against giving any offence to seeing people by unpleasant and unacceptable habits of speech, eating, bodily movement or anything else.

If a blind person can develop a way of handling a difficult situation with sufficient humour—not too much—and charm and tact, he can often prevent a crisis, ease the tension, and will have taken the first step in establishing a normal friendly relationship. There will be many embarrassing situations for every blind person, but if he can learn to cope with these in a confident, reassuring manner he will have done much to make his association with others happy and natural.

Missing the smile
The rather sad comment of a young man on his effort to seek acceptance at a mixed youth club is very typical of the problem the blind must face. ' Two sighted people can start a conversation by smiling at each other. You have to say something to a blind person before a conversation can begin! ' It is obviously difficult for a blind

person to make the first move in conversation, but often the embarrassment of others makes this necessary. Because he knows what helps and what hinders, it would be far more satisfactory if the blind person could make the first move and explain the few little practical matters which would make all the difference to both parties feeling at ease with each other. However, it is often not possible to do this before the embarrassing situation has arisen.

Often a seeing person does not realise that a blind person cannot know he is being addressed unless he is called upon by name, or given a tap on the shoulder. It can be equally embarrassing for a blind person to answer a question which was not intended for him, as to fail to reply when he has been addressed. The poor person who has thus failed to make contact with him will most likely be too shy to try again.

It is difficult for a blind person to catch the attention of someone he wishes to address in a room where there are a number of people talking. Even if he knows roughly where everyone is, there is quite an art in pitching his voice to be just right for the distance between himself and the person he wishes to address. This is something which a seeing person does without a thought, but a sensitive blind person often needs some courage to speak forth without any glance or gesture to help him. No wonder many go to the other extreme of monopolising conversation, and develop a rather loud and pompous manner, which is certain to get attention and drown anyone else who may have chosen exactly the same moment but a more subtle method of attracting attention.

Blind people are sometimes careless about forgetting the possible presence of others when they wish to say something of a private nature. They may choose the wrong moment, or not lower the voice sufficiently, because they are thinking only of themselves and not of the person to whom they wish to speak. If they make this mistake, at any age, they should be reminded of the need for more thought and care.

A delicate balance
There are dangers in a blind person's striving too much for independence. An intelligent blind girl, an Oxford graduate, said, 'I feel there are times when blind people can cause more embarrassment by trying to do something for themselves than by asking for help'. The same girl found that a great step towards normal friendship with

sighted people was to get them to talk to her about her blindness: ' Often these people forget I cannot see—they will say " when did you last see him? " or " was she looking well? " without having to apologise afterwards.'

This is a happy break-through to friendship. There is a delicate balance between too much concern and too little. Too much concern can be taken as a sort of patronage offensive to the blind: too little concern can be taken, just as easily, as either stupidity or lack of sympathy on the part of the sighted world. The aim of helping the blind in the community is to find—and achieve—balance.

The concern of most people to avoid embarrassing a blind person can often lead to more reticence than is wise. When a girl friend said to her: ' Perhaps it might be wise to wear another dress; that one is a bit grubby,' a blind girl's comment on this was that although it might have been hard for her friend to say it, it would have been much worse for her to have gone to a party in a dirty dress, where all the guests would have said: ' She can't help it, poor thing; she's blind.'

So many customs of the sighted world are visual—not holding your head down, looking at the person you wish to speak to, showing interest in what another says by looking in the right direction, wearing clothes and make-up that match, that are in the right style, and are chosen for the occasion.

These things the blind should welcome help with: only those who are disturbed by their blindness and who regard it as a handicap, will object to this kind of advice being given by those who know them well, when such advice is needed. Speaking of the great value of sighted friends to the unsighted, a girl said: ' Unobtrusive help is indeed something to be coveted. I did not know, because I could not see, that when one is sitting down, it is considered bad manners to stretch the feet out further than necessary. I was most grateful to the friend who summed up the courage to tell me this!'

The partially sighted
So far we have had the totally blind particularly in mind, but nearly everything that has been said applies, to some extent, to those with varying degrees of visual handicap. Because of the great variety in the kind of sight as well as in the degree of sight of these people, it is impossible to make general statements.

For educational purposes a distinction is made between the partially sighted and the partially blind: those who are technically classed as partially sighted are educated in special schools, but by sighted methods; the partially blind, some of whom may have a useful amount of sight, are usually unable to read much ordinary print and therefore need to be educated in schools for the blind, with braille as their medium for reading and writing. For our purpose in this chapter, we are using the term 'partially sighted' to cover both these categories.

Hiding their handicap

It is characteristic of these people that they usually take great delight in trying to hide their handicap. Often, the less sight such people have, the more they enjoy devising cunning means to prevent people from discovering that they are 'not normal'. Often those who go to great lengths to conceal their handicap suffer acutely from fears and dreads of 'being found out'. They are often quite seriously misunderstood and thought to be aloof and stand offish when they are too sensitive to explain that they cannot see to recognise people. It is usually girls and women who are most keen to hide their handicaps, probably for the simple reason that they wish to appear normally attractive to men, and not to be looked down upon by other women.

Not only the partially sighted, but most blind people who have memory of sight are conscious of the advantage they have over those who were born blind. Having learnt to walk and run as sighted infants, they are usually able to retain better poise and more natural movement as adults. Like the partially sighted they will go to great trouble to be thought normal, and enjoy a feeling of triumph when people do not notice that they cannot see. A boy blind since childhood said: 'Partially-sighted people are nearer to normal because they can see how people walk and do things. We refuse to walk slowly, even if we get hurt.'

Perhaps all we can say is that if they succeed, they have their reward, sometimes at considerable cost to themselves. If they slip up, they arouse at least temporary sympathy, which they probably hate so much that they make an even greater effort not to be caught out again.

A partially-sighted person who had come to live in a new place had been persuaded to join a women's group at the church. She had explained to the vicar's wife, but to no-one else, that she could not see well. She struggled for a while, attending meetings but dreading them, as she never recognised people she had spoken to at the last meeting, and seemed unable to make any progress in getting to know new friends. Finally she wrote explaining this to the vicar's wife and saying that she would not come to the meetings again. The vicar's wife replied that she had quite forgotten about the bad sight as it was so unnoticeable. What complex creatures we humans are, with our love of being noticed and our dread of being conspicuous; our desire to be cared for and our hatred of being patronised! This person had achieved her ambition—she had done particularly well; not only was her handicap not noticed, she had confessed it, and it had been forgotten. How delighted we would expect her to be! Yes, she could tell this as a good story to similarly handicapped friends, but deep down she felt a grudge against that vicar's wife for not caring enough to remember.

Someone who had met a partially-sighted person several times socially was rather puzzled that this person, who was reported to have bad sight, did not show it in any way. She moved about a room with no apparent difficulty, accepted drinks and food with no obvious fumbling and engaged in conversation in a normal and relaxed manner. The sighted woman was therefore shocked when she passed this apparently friendly person in the street one day and there was no glimmer of recognition. She was so surprised that she passed on without saying anything, but the next time they met, at the house of a mutual friend, she had the good sense to ask what she should have done. She was told: 'When you see me not seeing you, stop me, say hello to me, tell me who you are at once in case I don't recognise you, and then just treat me like anyone else.'

Because the partially sighted appear to be able to live full and independent lives, the strain they undergo in achieving this appearance of normality is rarely appreciated by others. A partially-sighted woman who is a capable housewife and teacher, writes of her difficulties, giving a picture of life as it is for most similarly handicapped people: 'The wise partially-sighted person, going to a church for the first time, takes a friend. She is then in a position—by entering the building behind her companion—to locate steps, commit them to memory, and so avoid falling up, down or over them at a future date!

'On walking up the aisle, she will know by the brightness and general colour, whether it is a "high" or "low" church. She will know whether it is well cared for mainly by the use of the olfactory sense—Does it smell sweet? or is there a musty, dusty odour? She will know if there are flowers, and if incense is used. All these things can be found out, but only partly through the use of vision. What she will not know—even if they include her next door neighbour—is the identity of any of the people present; they have no individual features, they are just this Sunday's congregation.

'The hymn board she can possibly read, if she is able to sit in a pew near enough; on the other hand she may pluck up courage to use a visual aid such as a small monocular. When the collection bag comes round she has to watch like a lynx, or that handle will appear under her nose from nowhere, or be sticking in her ribs, and a rather bored member of the congregation will be waiting patiently while she comes to her apparent senses and takes hold of it.

'Many church people think that when they have introduced her to half a dozen or so families, all will now be well: they feel that they have taken some extra trouble—which indeed they have—and now that little bridge is crossed. How wrong they are! The more active the church, the larger the congregation, and the more difficult for anyone who has very little vision, and has to recognise those around her by voice or clothes (until they get a new outfit) to sort out familiar, friendly faces! Her aim is to be as normal as possible. Here she gets into difficulties, as the general public still only thinks in terms of "blindness" and "short sight that can be cured by wearing the correct spectacles". It is largely ignorant of the many variations and degrees of what can be termed "part vision". This new-comer seems so normal that she is gradually left to her own devices and no-one notices that more and more she is alone, or if they do, they probably think that she likes it that way. Her lack of visual contact with strangers makes the making of fresh friends almost impossible. She is often unable to join fully in what goes on around; small incidents take place, which are not put into words by those with full sight, and these can completely change the course of a conversation. Either this girl says nothing, or she makes a remark which may come quite out of context. What is she to do? Be considered unsociable, or risk being thought a fool? If she asks for an explanation it spoils the spontaneity of the group; it is indeed often impossible to know *what* to ask. How rare and wonderful are those who take the trouble to know by instinct what a blind or partially-sighted person would miss in any given situation, and give just the right clue to make them feel part of the conversation, and thereby of the church community. How often is there a sudden burst of laughter—she joins in, not knowing what it is about, but being afraid of doing something incongruous, or being thought slow.

' If no special help is given, after a few weeks, or perhaps months, a partially-sighted person will feel that she is able to worship God as well at home, possibly listening to a wireless service on a Sunday. She is happier with her own hobbies and her few personal and usually close friends, rather than joining in church functions, which can be frustrating and impersonal. On the other hand she may feel that this is giving in, and plods on going to church each Sunday. After the service can be the worst time, as she watches members of the congregation talking in elated groups; they all seem so full of a happy, busy life, which in some way they are able to share, while she, with possibly a " good night " handshake from the vicar, steps bravely into the night to wend a precarious way home—the voices, the lights and the banging of car doors growing more faint as she picks her way along familiar pavements in the enveloping darkness.

' These good people do not mean to be unkind. They do not realise that she longs for social contact, for as she smilingly walks away she does not know who to speak to, and unless she is addressed by name does not know when she is spoken to! They do not realise that she is unable to pour out those unending cups of tea at church functions satisfactorily—because the surroundings are unfamiliar; that she could see jokes as well as they, and perhaps more subtle ones, if she had not missed that vital visual clue. That she would not have made that rather tactless remark to Mrs X last Sunday, if she had been able to see the expression on her face; she would have answered Mrs Y, if Mrs Y had thought to call her by her name. The life of a churchgoer is certainly hard when most faces look alike, and most details are gone.'

Who needs help

Having our attention drawn to an experience such as this should make us think. Perhaps it gives us a guilty feeling of how much more aware we should be of the needs of others. There are probably many people amongst us, at church, at work, in our social life, who are longing for understanding and sympathy, but for some strange reason are quite unable to convey their need to others. A handicapped person is really not being fair to those around him if he criticises them for not noticing his need when all the time he is busy contriving how to keep it hidden from them.

It is a good idea for a handicapped person who comes to live in a new place and who intends to become a member of a particular church, to write to the parish priest or minister. This might be followed by a conversation with him in which the particular handicap can be described and he can be told how much and just what kind of help would be appreciated. He can then have a word with a few suitable members of his congregation, so that the right kind of welcome and help will be available when the handicapped person first appears at church.

We have suggested earlier that the blind, knowing how they like other people to treat them, should take the initiative whenever they can, and show people in an understanding and tactful way what help they need and what they do not need. The partially sighted, too, would avoid much unhappiness if they could bring themselves to talk about themselves and explain their needs. They could still demonstrate, and perhaps more successfully in an understanding community, that they can do most things normally and that it is only in a few little, but quite important things that they need help.

A partially-sighted person who was fairly well known in her church community was asked if she would like to help the other women with the catering for a social occasion. The very sensible person who approached her said: ' We thought you might like to help, but we don't want to ask you to do anything that you would find difficult or embarrassing. You would probably prefer not to pour tea? ' This made the reply easy. ' I would probably make a mess either pouring or handing round tea. I find it rather embarrassing handing round food when I am not sure whether people are already eating or not. I could quite easily do some cooking beforehand, at home in my familiar surroundings, and I can wash up in any surroundings, so put me down for washing up! '

Many partially-sighted people remember how easy life was at school, when everyone understood and gave the necessary unobtrusive help without comment. The best way to make their adult life as relaxed and easy as their schooldays is to ensure that their seeing companions have the necessary knowledge to be able to show the same understanding.

Here are a few simple practical points which will avoid embarrassing a blind person by the wrong kind of approach:

Address him by name, or accompany your remarks by a light touch if you do not know his name.

Tell him who you are, unless you are quite certain that he will recognise your voice at once. It is difficult for a blind person to talk for long to someone he cannot recognise but feels he ought to know, and it is most tactless to ask him to guess who you are.

Tell him about such things as choice of food in a way which does not draw attention to his blindness—a little thought will show that it is just as easy to say ' Will you have an egg or a sardine sandwich?' as to say 'There are egg or sardine sandwiches'.

When leading a blind person always try to go first; do not push him into the unknown from behind. If he holds your arm in a normal manner he will probably be quite able to negotiate steps without anything being said.

Do not tell him he is wonderful; if he knows it already it is bad for him, and if he knows it not to be true, it is depressing.

Every handicap is unique because every individual's response to his own handicap is unique. A blind physiotherapist, speaking of her own patients, said: ' We have no right to assume that others ought to emulate our own efforts to overcome adversity. We must remind ourselves that everyone has a unique handicap to cope with, and we can help only from a sense of compassion—not cleverness.'

If blind and partially-sighted people are to take their place in society and to make a useful contribution to whatever situation they are in, they themselves, and the rest of the community, must care and think and take real trouble to understand each other, to give and take—and if there are mistakes, to forgive and forget at once.

In this chapter we have emphasised the difficulties that face visually handicapped people who live in a seeing community. It may give the impression that they are unable to enjoy life because they are continually frustrated in their contacts with others. This is only so for some people, sometimes. Many blind people are able to live full and active lives—enjoying the companionship of their colleagues at work, making happy homes for their families, and participating in a wide variety of social activities.

When preparing this chapter we asked many blind people for their experiences in coping with community life. We were grateful to those who took the trouble to write a contribution, but were disappointed that there were only a small number of replies, until we were reminded that people just get on with living and working—they do not stop to worry about their blindness. They forget that they have a handicap which may limit their activities, and they become simply a part of the community.

APPENDIX

Headmasters and parochial clergy in close contact with schools for blind children were consulted by questionnaire and letter at the beginning of the work undertaken by our group. The following is a short summary of the information and impressions received.

No-one would deny that the atmosphere of a residential school and the influence of those around him will make a tremendous mark upon the child who lives there. This is as important as anything he is taught. The living together, learning to adjust to environment, practising patience, understanding and tolerance of other people will only be learned from those with whom he comes into contact.

'Religious instruction in a residential setting means nothing to me unless it can be construed as a revealing of a living creed which gives inner serenity,' wrote one headmaster, and achievement of, or a striving towards this serenity is vital for those dealing with the special claims made upon them by handicapped children.

The life of a community twenty-four hours a day reflects the principles on which it is based. Many children come from homes where there is no tradition of Christian teaching and, therefore, the responsibility on the school for the upbringing of the child in religious matters is stressed. At the same time care must be exercised so that it does not become a question of school versus home.

Instruction will, of course, be given, but a dull and unenthusiastic approach must be avoided at all costs. In spite of their inability to see, children should not have to rely upon the teacher's voice. They learn better and enjoy it more if they take part. The use of tape recorders, tactile illustrations and drama makes the lessons so much more interesting. Thematic teaching enables the teacher to combine religious instruction with other subjects: history, geography, science and social studies. Stories of heroes, pioneers and missionaries have their place and with older children talks and discussions help to meet their need. Some go on to take 'O' Level and 'A' Level in R.I.

Great care should be taken in the choice of Biblical material as well as in Bible readings, even from the *New English Bible*. So much is better left until the children are able to appreciate it. They are more likely to respond if, at that age, it comes fresh and new to them.

Blind children, more than most, need guidance and security. Older children and adolescents often want someone with whom they can discuss their personal problems—not necessarily a member of the school staff. Reference has already been made to the contact between the school and the local churches, and in some instances the chaplain or the vicar of the church attended may be the right person to do this. In some parishes there is a woman worker on the staff who will be able to discuss problems with the girls. In many dioceses the Adviser in Children's Work is a woman who would willingly help in this way if no-one were available locally. Contact between the chaplain and the parish clergy of the child's home parish is obviously most useful, as is his contact with the chaplain of the institutes of further training to which the child goes.

Although schools have contact with the churches, corporate worship is an integral part of school life. This should be varied, although the framework may remain fairly steady. The difficulty is to retain the spirit of real worship and devotion and not to allow it to become merely a matter of routine; it can so easily lose its impact and become boring. In some schools children not only take part but on occasions organise the whole service. Many have a school choir, which is a great delight to the children; they enjoy singing church music and extracts from the great oratorios. They often visit churches in the locality in order to sing.

This is one way of giving them an opportunity of doing something for others: an important fact for seeing people to realise. It helps the children to feel more adequate, more useful and gives them a greater sense of being needed. It must be remembered, too, that they give practical help by holding concerts in order to raise funds for such organisations as Oxfam. Through this connection with local churches, many of them are finding a way of worship.

It is important for the young blind child to be attached to one particular Church. When he is older he may wish and may even be encouraged to get to know something of other Christian denominations, possibly of other religions. Meantime it is of vital importance for the child to come to know the clergy of the church he attends. A distant voice reading from the Bible or saying prayers means little or nothing to the child, but a voice which he can recognise as belonging to the vicar, whom he meets regularly in church and/or school and whom he knows personally, means infinitely more. The same kind of personal relationship is needed with seeing adults with whom he may come in contact. It is also through such relationships that seeing adults will learn to recognise where practical help may be given to the blind and how to draw them into church activities. They need to remember that the blind have much to give and should not always be on the receiving end; they will discover when and how the blind may be called upon to give of their time and talents. More needs to be done to establish this sort of relationship between the church and the home as well as between the church and the school. It would be helpful if seeing adults would realise that blind children need to be treated naturally and that it is not necessary or wise to be over-solicitous towards them.

Although all blind children are in boarding-schools, many are able to go home at the weekend. In this case there need be no loss of contact between the child and his own church at any time of the year. Integration with the parish community is, therefore, best achieved through the child's own family. This responsibility of the parents is often lacking and then it is harder to make contact with the blind than it would be with a seeing child.

Where the child does not go home for the weekend integration into the parish community for term-time only is not easy, though successful attempts have been made. If the parents request that the child should attend any particular church, he is usually allowed to do so. Otherwise the children normally attend services together until they are older, when they attend the local church of their choice in the neighbourhood. On some Sundays, often alternately, the service is held in the school.

In one school those who are confirmed attend a Family Communion service on Sunday. Adult members of the congregation have assumed responsibility for collecting blind communicants by car, sitting with them and helping them up to the altar rail without fuss. They all go on to the breakfast afterwards—hot dogs and coke. At this school too, confirmation preparation has been a great success with one or two blind children to groups of about twenty-four sighted children. They are given braille copies of the Communion service for a Confirmation present.

In another school those who are confirmed attend a Communion service at the parish church on a weekday once a fortnight. This gives those weekly boarders whose families do not attend church an opportunity to make their Communion with their school friends.

At the same time it does not prevent others from attending with their own families in the home parish on Sunday.

Provision is also made for resident children (infant and junior) to attend Sunday school, and on the whole they are integrated into classes of seeing children. (This is what the blind seem to prefer themselves, although additional skill is required of the teacher. This is an important factor to be considered.) In one parish the children of 7–12 from the blind school are integrated with seeing children in Sunday school. The school duty staff bring them and they are met by church teachers and children who guide them in—only a few blind children are in each seeing class. Comments make it clear that blind children, though often less intelligent than most sighted children, are in fact much more communicative and very retentive in memory.

Other outside activities with younger children are difficult to arrange. It is perhaps easier for the ' outside ' to come to the school when this is possible. In fact schools do invite members of the local churches to their own functions, such as Open Days, plays, concerts and socials. In one school the vicar has a voluntary class of juniors once a week for half an hour, mainly of children who remain at school at weekends. This contact is considered to be invaluable and, it is thought, could be extended.

Over a number of years various ways have been tried of integrating the senior boys and girls into Youth Clubs, with varying degrees of success. It was more successful in the old days of ballroom dancing but now that so many activities need sight it is more difficult. At some schools members of outside Youth Clubs come and help with evening activities, but even then after a year or more friendships between blind and sighted are usually only superficial.

The more mutual contact there can be between church and school and church and home, the better will be the understanding and the more easily will personal relationships be formed. It is these which are going to make the blind person, whatever his age, feel that he is cared for, that he belongs to and can become a full member of a Christian community.

Bibliography

Psychology
The Blind in School and Society, by T. D. Cutsforth, American Foundation for the Blind, 15 West 16th Street, New York 11. 1951. In some ways this is a very critical book indicating failings in our system. It may be biased, but it is a valuable book and does indicate some of the problems faced by blind children.

The World of the Blind, by P. Villey, Duckworth. This is quite a classic and makes very interesting reading. It was originally written in French. Villey himself was a blind man and the book does indicate how a blind child comes to terms with the world around him.

The Emotional and Social Adjustment of Blind Children, by Dr Kellmer Pringle, *Educational Research, vi, no.* 2, 1964. An excellent study which includes extracts from all the important recent works on the emotional needs of older blind children.

Sociology
Blind Children in Family and Community, by M. B. Spencer, OUP, 1960. This useful book shows how blind children can be helped to develop as normally as possible in their everyday activities at home and in the community. The emphasis is on young blind children.

Blindness, by the Rev. Thomas J. Carroll, Little, Toronto, 1961. A realistic approach to the problem of blindness, particularly with older people. Of great value to all those who are trying to understand blind people.

Our Blind Children, by Berthod Lowenfeld, Blackwell Scientific Publications, 1956. The author, who is a knowledgeable student of blind children, deals with their needs in their home environment in particular.

If You make a Noise, I can't See, by Lucy Lunt, Victor Gollancz, 1965. Miss Lunt was the head of a Sunshine Home when she wrote this very readable book about young blind children.

Health

The Science of Seeing, by Ida Mann, Harmondsworth, 1946. Now issued by Penguin. A fascinating book on vision and eye diseases; the illustrations are excellent and the book itself has become quite a classic.

Autobiographies

My Eyes have a Cold Nose, by H. Chevigny, Michael Joseph, 1947.
To Catch an Angel, by R. Russell, Cassell, 1963.
There was Light, by Lusseyran, Heinemann, 1964.

Without any doubt anyone interested in the blind should read these three exceptionally well written autobiographies. In the last book, *There was Light,* there is more excitement and drama than in any thriller. Lusseyran was a blind man engaged in the resistance movement in France amongst many other things.

ORGANISATIONS

Association for the Education and Welfare of the Partially Sighted, George Auden School, Bell Hill, Northfield, Birmingham 31

Founded in 1948. Membership composed of persons interested in any way in the problems of the partially sighted.

British Wireless for the Blind, 226 Great Portland Street, London W1

This Fund provides radio sets free on permanent loan to those people in Great Britain who are in need of them.

College of Teachers for the Blind, Royal School for the Blind, Westbury-on-Trym, Bristol

Founded in 1907 as an Association of professional workers, the College's professional qualifications are recognised both nationally and internationally.

Deaf/Blind and Rubella Children's Association, 63 Horn Lane, Woodford Green, Essex

Started in 1955 by parents of children with a combined sight and hearing handicap caused by maternal rubella (German measles), the Association is made up of parents and professional workers concerned with welfare and education.

Guide Dogs for the Blind Association, 83–89 Uxbridge Road, Ealing W5

The Association undertakes the training and supplying of dog guides to the blind.

The Jewish Blind Society, House for the Jewish Blind, 1 Craven Hill, Lancaster Gate W2

This Society, established in 1819, ministers to the needs of the Jewish blind and partially sighted throughout the United Kingdom.

National Association of Workshops for the Blind, Inc., 8–22 Curtain Road EC2 (General Welfare). Tadcaster Road, Dringhouses, York (Registered Offices)

This Association is made up of approved agencies conducting workshops and/or home workers' schemes for the blind in the United Kingdom.

National Federation of the Blind in the United Kingdom, 20 Canon Close, London SW20

The objects of this Federation include the organising of blind persons who are capable of engaging in useful professions and industrial occupations and the betterment of conditions of non-seeing people.

National League of the Blind, 262 Langham Road, London N15

This League was founded for the purpose of obtaining State responsibility for the employment, at adequate wages, of all sightless persons who have been trained in trades and professions; and, for those who cannot be trained, adequate pensions.

National Library for the Blind, 35 Great Smith Street, London SW1—Northern Branch at 5 St John Street, Manchester 3

Private readers, public libraries and institutes can borrow free of charge and post free, embossed type books (including music) from a library of over 300,000 volumes.

Royal National Institute for the Blind, 224 Great Portland Street, London W1

Concerned with every aspect of blindness, the Institute includes among its services educational facilities for the blind child at every stage of childhood (Parents' Unit, nursery schools, schools for children with additional handicaps, grammar schools, a vocational guidance centre, and schools for technical training); book and periodical production in Braille and Moon; a talking book library; Braille and tape students' libraries; rehabilitation and training of the newly-blinded; and the development and provision of aids and apparatus for the blind.

73

St Dunstan's (For Service War Blinded), 191 Marylebone Road, London NW1
Training, care and help with employment of war-blinded men and women. Permanent home for the sick and infirm.

North Regional Association for the Blind, Headingley Castle, Headingley Lane, Leeds

Southern Regional Association for the Blind, 14 Howick Place, London SW1

Western Regional Association for the Blind, 39 East Street, Newton Abbot, Devon

SCOTLAND

Scottish National Federation for the Welfare of the Blind, 39 St Andrew's Street, Dundee
Federates all the organisations and local authorities in Scotland.

Scottish Board of the Jewish Blind Society, 16 Newark Drive, Glasgow SW

Society for Welfare and Teaching of the Blind, 4 Coates Crescent, Edinburgh 3. (Covers Edinburgh and the South-East of Scotland)

WALES AND MONMOUTHSHIRE

Wales and Monmouthshire Council for the Blind, Llaindelyn, 31 Folland Road, Garnant, Ammanford, Carms.

NORTHERN IRELAND

Ulster Society for Promoting the Education of the Deaf, the Dumb and the Blind, Jordanstoun School, 85 Jordanstoun Road, Newtownabbey, Co. Antrim

Founded in 1831, this Society includes in its objects the education of blind and partially-sighted children of all religious denominations.

Belfast Association for the Employment of the Industrious Blind, Lawnbrook Avenue, Belfast, 13

EIRE

Irish Association for the Blind, 8 North Great George's Street, Dublin

National Council for the Blind of Ireland, 11 Molesworth Street, Dublin

National League of the Blind of Ireland, 35 Gardiner Place, Dublin

CHANNEL ISLES

Guernsey Association for the Education and Welfare of the Necessitous Blind, La Porte, St Saviour's, Guernsey

Jersey Society for the Education and Welfare of the Necessitous Blind, Hillway, Rue de la Blanche Pierre, St Lawrence, Jersey

COMMONWEALTH

Royal Commonwealth Society for the Blind, 39 Victoria Street, London SW1

Founded in 1950, the objects of this Society are to stimulate official and voluntary action, and to take a lead in the movement to promote the welfare, education, and employment of the blind, and to prevent blindness, in the emergent countries of the Commonwealth (i.e. apart from the UK, Canada, Australia and New Zealand).